the 7
Signals of
MEANING

HOW WRITERS CAN SAY
WHAT THEY MEAN

ROBERT PICKFORD

Kendall Hunt
publishing company

Cover image © Shutterstock, Inc.

Kendall Hunt
publishing company

www.kendallhunt.com
Send all inquiries to:
4050 Westmark Drive
Dubuque, IA 52004-1840

To Mariann Grasela, whose advice and encouragement helped make this book such a pleasure to write.

Table of Contents

Preface

Ask almost anyone to name the basics of good writing, and "good grammar" or even "grammatically correct sentences" will probably get onto the list, probably near the top. At work, many people complain about the sentence-writing skills of their co-workers. Employers complain that they see employees and job applicants producing writing filled with grammatical errors, and college professors complain that they have students who cannot write well enough to produce error-free sentences and doubt that such students are adequately prepared for intellectually demanding courses. Colleges often place many of their new students in basic courses, for instance English-as-a Second-or-Other-Language courses for students whose first language was not English. Courses with titles like "English Review," "Developmental English," "College English," or "Basic Composition" offer first-language speakers (and non-first language speakers who have progressed to first-language level) instruction in writing sentences, paragraphs, or essays or, in some cases, all three in one course. A good general term for these types of entry-level courses might be "basic writing."

Teaching students in basic writing classes has taught me one essential truth about writing sentences. Only about half of students in a classroom can learn the grammatical rules of Standard Written English well enough to consistently see when a sentence violates one of them, and far fewer of them see how to apply those rules to proofreading their own writing. In my own students' writing, I have seen their frustration in gaining control over types of errors that appear again and again in their sentences. In searching for an effective way of teaching writers to eliminate sentencing errors, I drew upon my reading of composition methodology and some prior experience in discourse analysis and have identified a set of seven ways writers signal their actual intentions in their sentences. I use those seven signals (quantity, time, identity, location, transaction, sequence, and relation) to introduce inexperienced writers to the basic truth that every sentence they write has an intended meaning and any sentencing error that sends a mixed signal of intent distorts that meaning. I introduced this approach into my Basic Composition course in a summer session class a couple of years ago and, based on the encouraging results, have fine-tuned it and use it regularly in my Basic Composition as well as my Reading and Composition courses here at San Diego Mesa College.

At this point, it bears mentioning that these seven signals of intent aren't simply another method of alerting students to particular types of sentencing errors and then directing them to edit on their own time (or, in the case of Reading and Composition students, simply directing them to a handbook to aid them in figuring out what went wrong and how to fix it). Instead, what I'm proposing here is a system for writers and their readers to dialog about the intended meaning of a sentence and how to more fully realize the intention. In responding to my own students' writing, notating a sentence whose meaning is unclear in the margins of a student's graded paper begins a dialog on the nature of each particular mixed signal and its role in thwarting the writer's intended meaning. That dialog supports the method for discovering the intended meaning in a student's sentences on that piece of writing as well as any writing that comes later.

I learned the value of dialog not just by working with an editor when I wrote for a small magazine three years ago or even in working together with Holly Paige, the Project Coordinator at Kendall Hunt, on my vision for this book. I first visualized it while I was still a student myself, tutoring my fellow students, first at the San Diego City College English Center, then at the Washington State University Writing Center, and more recently while directing the San Diego Mesa College Writing Center. That dialog between a reader and a writer seldom involved the nomenclature of the English language or the recitation of grammatical rules. It had occurred to me that the more insight and skill I picked up in helping writers write better sentences, the more the conversation focused on what they intended to say and how it could come to the page more clearly. That epiphany was the inspiration for this book.

In teaching composition courses, students in two particular courses seemed to benefit the most from thinking of their writing at the sentence-level as ways of signaling their intended meaning. Students in the class below the first-year Composition course that leads to the baccalaureate, a "pre-first year" lower-level writing course that appears under various names in colleges and universities, Developmental Composition, or Basic Composition, and so on, seem to progress rapidly and with greater confidence in writing better sentences with fewer errors. Most of the students who succeed in a basic-level composition course go on to take first-year Composition at their college or university, and whether they first needed to take the basic-level college writing course or not, these students also benefit from an approach focused on their intended meaning in a sentence, even if they also use a writer's handbook, the kind of "fix-it" guide that appears with other first-year composition texts on the shelves on college bookstores nearly everywhere. Students often think of passing a course in Basic Composition as one of the first "hoops" they will need to jump through as they move year to year through their degree programs. Students may not have to jump so high if they work with their teachers and each other in focusing more on what they meant instead of learning the correct term for what they did wrong.

The project of developing the seven ways writers signal meaning never would have amounted to much without countless conversations with student writers, writing tutors, and writing teachers. The staff, faculty, and students who tutor students in the Washington State University Writing Lab and the Mesa College Writing Center deserve specific mention here because our discussions about helping frustrated writers got me thinking and developing the unconventional approach in the chapters that follow. My students who struggled to write more error-free sentences, so they could say what they meant and mean what they said, also deserve recognition because they taught me so much.

Introduction for Students

Why this Book?

This is a book about sentences. It gets at the basics of writing in ways that other books on writing have not. This happens for two reasons. One is the likelihood that the authors of other books believed that writing better sentences was just one skill out of many readers needed to learn, and the basics of sentencing got a just few pages of attention before those textbooks went onto the business of forming a paragraph and even organizing an essay. The other reason is that many books on writing simply break sentence-level errors down into categories, present examples of the errors, state a rule that applies, and show how that particular error should be fixed. Naturally the success of such an approach to improving writing at the sentence-level hinges on learning rules, lots of them--rather than discovering the intention that led to the sentence in the first place.

Whenever they get back their writing assignments, students in college courses that require those kinds of textbooks typically see a kind of code in the margins, initials like "r-o" (for "run-on sentence") or editing symbols like ∧ to alert the writer that a word is missing. The student writer then has to decipher the meaning of the abbreviation or symbol, look up the term it stands for, read the rule, and then somehow apply it. That kind of repeated fixing of sentencing errors is useful only in very limited ways because sentences come in response to an unlimited variety of thoughts and situations.

How this Book is Different

As a system for spotting, fixing, and avoiding sentence-level errors, the *7 Ways Writers Signal Meaning* offers a very different approach than the one used by most textbooks on sentence-writing. In brief, this book presents a system based on what we might call the "ARS" principle—the idea that a good tool should be adaptable, reliable, and simple. The plain truth is that *7 Ways Writers Signal Meaning* is a different kind of writing text.

- It doesn't require much (if any) instruction on the nomenclature of Standard Written English.
- It doesn't require decoding editing symbols, then figuring out how a rule applies, and finally attempting to put the rule into practice by fixing the error.
- The "expert" is not the reader who spots mistakes, but the writer who best knows what he or she meant to say and uses a reader's questions and responses to make a sentence's intended meaning clear.
- The focus is on sentences.
- The system is jargon-free and relies on common sense and every-day terms.

What the Seven Signals Are and How They Work

There are many ways a writer signals the meaning of what he or she is writing. Of course, there is a specific meaning of a sentence that serves the purpose of communicating a writer's thought on a topic. Also, that particular sentence has its place in a paragraph. For the sentence to fulfill either of those needs, though, that writer's thought needs a sentence that expresses the thought the way he or she meant it. All the ways someone can signal to the reader what he or she meant can be broken down to just seven different ways a writer may signal meaning in a sentence: quantity, time, identity, location, transaction, sequence, and relation. Not every sentence a person writes uses or even needs all seven, but most sentences use at least one or two. As a "system" for accurately expressing a thought, looking at how well a sentence signals meaning has several advantages:

- The seven signals of meaning don't replace the grammatical rules, terms, or the conventions of usage. This is a system for applying those rules, terms, and conventions in a writerly way—as opposed to starting with the rules and then trying to write something meaningful.
- The signals can be learned and used either with or without the "rulebook," namely the "writer's handbook" or other classroom texts that rely on those rules, terms, and conventions to show the way to correcting sentences.
- Even if a writer may not actually know which rule applies or even exactly how to apply a grammatical rule, more clearly signaling of his or her intended meaning in a sentence may solve a grammatical problem anyway.
- A reader plays a role, but as one who asks questions and offers suggestions about a writer's intended meaning.
- Any fluent English speaker who reads and writes well can fill the role as a reader, though a more experienced reader or trained tutor might use the seven signals system in more adaptable way.

How Readers Make a Difference

It is safe to say that people who write usually imagine a reader of their writing. In some cases that reader is actually someone the writer knows—a friend, a classmate, a teacher, a prospective employer, or any person whose identity causes the creation of a particular piece of writing in the first place. In other cases, the identity of the reader is unknown—the public, hundreds or even thousands of fellow students, anonymous coworkers—in other words, the many anonymous readers of a public piece of writing. It is also safe to say that people who write do not often appreciate the reader's role in the early stages of a piece of writing. If a writer is willing to allow a reader onto the page well before the writing is completed and perfect in every way, that reader can play a role in helping the writer complete and perfect the writing.

If this seems strange, think for a minute about the possible benefits brought by readers who arrive onto the page early. The best move a writer can make if he or she wants to write more error-free sentences is sitting down with someone who doesn't just fix the errors but instead works with the writer as a curious reader. This is how a writing center tutor or a patient and thoughtful friend who happens to be a good writer can help. As a former college writing center tutor, someone whose job it was to read the writing of others before the intended readers would see it, it became evermore clear to me over the years that dialog about a writer's intended meaning in a sentence was a useful alternative to what entry-level college students often saw on their returned writing assignments. Marks on papers often identify errors but don't always say how to fix them or how to spot them next time. The seven signals system helps readers learn to do both by making readers a writer's resource that supports the writer's intended meaning.

How the Book is Organized

After a short introduction for teachers who are planning to use this book, seven chapters define and explain the seven signals of meaning. Each way of signaling meaning (quantity, time, identity, location, transaction, sequence, and relation) gets a chapter that explains what it is, what happens when the signal gets mixed in a sentence, and what some likely solutions look like. Each chapter has four sections, the first on how the signal can get mixed and unmixed in basic sentences as well as expanded sentences, a second section on some ways writers can get help finding solutions through dialog with a reader, a third section that offers writers a "microlearning" moment for making the most of a reader's feedback, and finally an opportunity for readers to get some practice at spotting a writer's mixed signals.

Three appendices in the back of this book contain some materials that writers and teachers of writers may find useful. Appendix one explains things that aren't words but those marks on which words rely, namely punctuation. Its use also flows from those same ways writers attempt to convey clear meaning. In appendix two, readers will find proofreading tools that are configured as "decision trees," an alternate way of visualizing the seven signals, and a reference sheet that sorts the standard grammatical terms by the seven signals. In appendix three, readers will also see the solutions to the signaling problems displayed in each chapter's self-test.

As a reader who is also a writer, you will see an approach to sentencing drawn from the experience of not just a writing teacher but students like you who came here hoping for an adaptable, reliable, and simple system that works. Take a few minutes to glance through this book to see how it is organized, and what the content of each chapter looks like. This book also presents dialog between readers and writers and encourages them to keep using the dialog long after the talking has stopped.

Introduction for Teachers

The premise of this book is that grammar and usage are dependent upon intended meaning, not the other way around. As someone who tutored student writers and later directed a college writing center, what seemed far more useful than requiring students to either do repetitive exercises or retain the terms, rules, and exceptions of English usage and then apply them was an observation that the more student writers could learn to clearly signal their intended meaning in sentence after sentence, the fewer errors remained in their sentences. That observation led to a shift in tutoring technique to one that used an adaptable, reliable, and simple system. Over several sessions with tutors, or even by the end of a single session in more than a few cases, students learned how to significantly reduce their sentence-level errors as a by-product of clarifying their intended meaning. They learned that in composing sentences, writers signal their intended meaning in seven ways: quantity, time, identity, location, transaction, sequence, and relation.

This is neither another writer's handbook on the do's and don'ts of writing sentences nor a workbook on sentencing skills in any traditional sense. Handbooks seldom help even half of the students in a writing class spot and fix errors, let alone help them understand how they made a certain type of error in the first place. That shouldn't be surprising since there is only so much students who use handbooks will have learned. There are eight parts of speech, each one with its own rules;

seven types of nouns; six types of pronouns; three types of articles; three types and four forms of sentences; two types of conjunctions; three forms and eight types of adverbs; two forms and three types of prepositions and particles; three forms, two types, and two classes of adjectives; and two types, six basic tenses, and three forms of verbs. If one assumes that students need to know all eight parts of speech, understand their rules for usage, be able to recognize any sentence in which one of the rules is broken, and then know how to fix the sentence, those students will need to have elephantine memories and still not be too intimidated to put their thoughts on a page. Workbooks likewise only help a little because they tend to focus on particular sentencing problems and then offer sets of remedies and repetitive exercises to build students' ability to adapt what they have been practicing to their own sentences. Neither handbooks nor workbooks go very far giving students the sentencing skills they need.

The approach here is different—a system students can learn for putting the rules, terms, and conventions of Standard Written English into practice *without* necessarily learning them at first. By working at seeing and identifying their intended meaning in seven ways, writers can see their sentencing improve *without* having to know very many grammatical terms and sentencing conventions by name.

Not every sentence a student writes is intended to do this in all seven ways, but in the moment of composing a sentence, a writer signals quantity, time, identity, location, transaction, sequence, or relation. Integrating this system into your own writing pedagogy may inspire you to try new ways to respond to student writing. For instance, when identifying one of your own students' mixed signal of meaning in one of his or her sentences, you might see what happens when you simply identify the mixed signal in the margins and later explain the signal to the student verbally while referencing pages from this text. Alternately, posing a question to promote the kind of dialog about intended meaning could lead to a better sentence and, with later writing and dialog, better future sentences.

Samples of such questions appear at the beginnings of the chapters and are demonstrated in the second section of each chapter in "Finding Solutions through Dialog with a Reader."

How This Book is Organized

The book's chapters define and explain the seven signals of meaning. Each way of signaling meaning gets its own chapter, and each chapter has four sections.

The first section, "What Can Happen When [the signal] Gets Mixed in a Sentence," includes within it "Samples of Basic Sentences and Solutions," "Samples of Expanded Sentences and Solutions," and "Samples of Questions, Directions, and Exclamations"; two other chapter sections, "Finding Solutions through Dialog with a Reader"; "Microlearning Tips for Using what a Reader Has Seen"; and a self-test section, where students can assess their understanding of the signal and actively reflect on their own dialog with a reader.

The appendices in the back of this book contain some materials that writers and teachers of writers may find useful. Appendix one focuses on punctuation's role in signaling intended meaning. In appendix two, readers will find proofreading tools that are configured as "decision trees," an alternate way of finding mixed signals, and a reference sheet that sorts the standard grammatical terms by the seven signals. In appendix three, readers will also see the solutions to the signaling problems displayed in each chapter's self-test.

While each chapter includes paragraph-length self-tests on each of the seven signals, the focus of this book is sentences. It stands to reason that students need to construct paragraphs with their sentences, but learning to build better sentences is arguably more challenging and takes longer than learning to construct solid paragraphs.

This might be a good time for English instructors to consider their colleagues who do not teach writing but teach in subject areas that require students to write. College faculty in most academic disciplines complain about their students' competence in sentence-level writing far more often than they take issue with their students' paragraphing.

On that note, faculty in those disciplines might see the seven signals as not just for English teachers and their students. Accounting, anthropology, art history, biology, business, engineering, history, nursing, psychology, and sociology are all subject areas requiring writing that accurately communicates what the student means. It follows that this book may be a useful addition to the book list for a class in one of those disciplines.

Quantity

Do you mean one or more than one?

The "How Many" Problem

The problem starts with casual conversation. For instance, we tend to use "their" when we probably mean an unknown person, as in "someone left their lights on." But "some<u>one</u> is one person, and "their" indicates something belongs to "them," not an individual. We probably do this in conversation because it takes less time and thought. Saying "someone left his or her lights on" takes more time (since "their" has one less syllable than "his or her"), and it's easier to say "their" than it is to stop and think whether the situation could involve only the male, female, or either gender.

Instead of signaling too many, a different sample does not signal quite enough: "There's a lot of directions to follow." More than one specific direction requires "<u>There are</u> a lot of directions," of course, and spoken expressions like this don't always seem odd until they appear in written form. There are other instances when mix-ups in quantity happen in this chapter.

When a sentence of yours does not clearly signal whether you meant one or many in a sentence, the signal of quantity seems mixed up. Because you need to clearly signal whether you mean one or more than one by choosing the right words or words' endings that signal the quantity you mean, this chapter will show you what some of those words or words' endings are as it reveals how mixed signals of quantity typically happen, what the solutions look like, how a reader can aid a writer in seeing mixed signals of quantity, and how you can develop an eye for seeing and repairing them. Take a few minutes to preview this chapter's four sections, which you will see **numbered and titled in bold**.

1. What Can Happen when a Quantity Signal Gets Mixed in a Sentence

Mixed signals of quantity can happen in any kind of sentence, ranging from basic or relatively simple sentences to somewhat more involved sentences that read as expanded versions of basic sentences. When a writer doesn't clearly signal quantity in a basic sentence, the mixed signal is often easy to see.

Samples of Basic Sentences and Solutions

One of the most common ways quantity gets mixed is a good place to start:

Everyone has their different job description.

People mix up the quantity they mean in sentences like this one regularly, especially in casual conversation, and if English is their first language, this kind of trouble can show up like the "someone" statement illustrated in this chapter's first paragraph. In the same way, the quantity the writer had in mind is not clear because "everyone" actually means "every one of them," in other words, just one person at a time, while "their" means more than one person, indicating that "they" have a job description. If the person who typed the sentence actually meant more than one person, the solution could involve revising the sentence to read as either "<u>People</u> <u>have</u> their different job descriptions," or "<u>Individuals</u> <u>each</u> <u>have</u> <u>a</u> different job description."

Alternately, the solution that also could work is "Everyone has <u>his or her</u> different job description." Even though "everyone," "everybody," "anybody," "nobody," and even "somebody" and "someone" all mean just one individual, it's not surprising when a writer makes the mistake of thinking that one of these words means more than one person. If one of these has gotten you wondering how it can really only mean one person, simply compare it by first putting it one way then the other: "Everyone <u>are</u> here" just does not sound right while "Everyone <u>is</u> here" sounds like the right quantity signal. The same test works for "everybody," "anybody," "anyone," "nobody," "somebody," and "someone."

The next few samples have less to do with casual conversation and more to do with how people mix signals of quantity when they write:

The organization consist of members as young as 13 and as old as 50.

Since the sentence reads "<u>the</u> organization," the writer needs to decide whether that signals that the subject of the sentence is just one organization or not. If just one organization is the intended quantity, it gets mixed with "consist," and "the simple solution is changing it to "consist<u>s</u>."

The next sample looks deceptively different but is actually somewhat similar, with "one" as the key to the solution:

I agree that one can be a genius in one's owns head.

While "one," "genius," and "head" are things whose quantity needs to be clear, "own" just describes "head." As a describing word, "own" cannot be used to signal quantity (unlike other describing words like "many" and "few"). The solution then is "I agree that one can be a genius in one's <u>own</u> head." The question of where to add an "s" oftentimes confuses the writer of a sentence like this, so just as "own," requires changing the word's ending by deleting the "s" to un-mix the quantity, the opposite thing happens in this next sentence with "rots" instead of "rot":

Some people say that either video games or television rot the brain.

When someone writes a sentence with "either" and then "or," that usually signals one at a time (much like the use of "everyone"). While "video games" is more than one game, television is just one because here it means something abstract—a medium of mass communication—rather than just a lot of televisions. If the sentence's writer did in fact mean them both separately, the second one, "television" determines the quantity signal: "Some people say that either video games or television rots the brain."

On the other hand, the quantity signal goes the other way when it comes to "teach" instead of "teaches" in this next sentence:

Video games teaches us about triumph over adversity.

This is because "video games" still mean more than one game, and this time, there is no single second item (like "television") to switch the signal: "Video games teach us about triumph over adversity."

The sentence below sends a mixed signal of quantity for a different reason, namely that the solution depends on what the writer does with "each," "have" and "set" as they all signal quantity in this next sentence:

Each society and culture have a different set of social expectations.

Either "Society and culture have different sets of social expectations" or "Each society and culture has a different set of social expectations," would fix the mix-up. As always, the choice between these solutions depends on whether the sentence's writer meant "society" and "culture" together or separately.

The next sample sentence's quantity signals are mixed for a similar reason:

The software designers are all from a different background.

Since the quantity of "designers" does not match the quantity of "background," the writer of the sentence would need to make the quantities match to create a solution: "The software designers are all from different backgrounds," (or) "The software designers are each from a different background."

The solution to the next one lies in basic arithmetic:

One of the classmate suggested that we have a bake sale to raise money for diabetes research.

As long as the person who composed this sentence meant more than one classmate was present, the solution is pretty straightforward. The phrase, "one of the" indicates one person suggesting as one person among many people, in other words, as part of a group: "One of the classmates suggested that we have a bake sale to raise money for diabetes research."

On the other hand, some words need no quantity signal themselves because they are not "countable":

We decided not to travel by the bus to school.

We took the public transportation instead.

Both "bus" and "public transportation" mean something too abstract to count, not a single bus like the "the school bus" or "the Route 9 Bus," and not a single form of public transportation, like a bus or a train (or more specifically, the bus or the train to mean a certain one). The writer didn't need to say "the" bus, unless the sentence gets revised as "We decided not to take the bus to school," which is a specific bus. Otherwise, those solutions involve making it clear that the mode of travel was something in the general, abstract sense: "We decided not to travel by bus to school." "We took public transportation instead."

Samples of Expanded Sentences and Solutions

Adding a bit more to a basic sentence expands what it describes even though it still needs to clearly signal the quantity the writer meant. This first expanded sentence resembles the two samples above since it contains a "non-countable" term like "public transportation," a word that is almost always singular. In this case, the sample contains a non-countable word that is almost always more than one:

If people are not aware of their surrounding, their perspective is limited because they did not explore their environment.

Of course, the only possible solution is "surroundings" The word is always plural when used this way.

This next one has a mixed quantity signal because it contains a countable word:

It is not possible for a group of people who know nothing about topography to reach the expedition's base camp since they would be unprepared for the type of terrain indicated on the map.

If the writer really meant "a group," there would be an "it," not a "they" later in the sentence, plus another change in quantity: "It is not possible for a group of people who knows nothing about topography to reach the expedition's base camp since it would be unprepared for the type of terrain indicated on the map." Alternately, if the sentence's writer did mean to use "they" and also "group," the solution would be "It is not possible for members of a group who know nothing about topography to reach the expedition's base camp since they would be unprepared for the type of terrain indicated on the map."

This next sample has the same kind of problem:

Since business conditions have worsened, video game developers are in a period of pursuing only new projects that meet the demand of consumers.

The way this sentence is written makes it clear that the first solution is either "projects" or "project": "Since business conditions have worsened, video game developers are in a period of pursuing only new projects that meet the demands of consumers," or one project at a time, as in "only a new project that meets the demands of consumers." Also the "s" needs to go onto "demand" unless the end of the sentence had been written to use it as a non-countable term, like "public transportation": "only new projects that meet consumer demand." Notice that "consumer" would lose its quantity signal in such a solution because it would become a describing word.

This next one's solution also depends on the quantity its writer had in mind:

For example, playing video games tend to be addictive, and many gaming situations may tempt the player to copy behavior of what they are watching.

Did the one who wrote this sentence mean to say that "video games tend to be addictive, and many gaming situations may tempt the players to copy behavior of what they are watching" or is another quantity intended? Once the subject of the sentence is "playing," an activity counted as singular, "tend" would need to become "tends" to clearly signal quantity in this part of the sentence, and of course, the matter of one player or more than one as "they" still needs clearing up: "For example, playing video games tends to be addictive, and many gaming situations may tempt players to copy behavior of what they are watching." If the writer meant only one player, the quantity signal would have to change to become "For example, playing video games tends to be addictive, and many gaming situations may tempt the player to copy behavior of what he or she is watching."

This next sample may seem familiar. As in the "everyone" issue in one of the samples of basic sentences earlier in this chapter, "everybody" is a kind of shorthand for "every individual person," so a reader would assume that the intended quantity signal is "a stranger":

Everybody has a different job description, is not employed at the same location, and is stranger, so many game designers do much of their work alone.

As a "one person" solution, that quantity would need to be consistent all the way to the last part of the sentence: "Everybody has a different job description, is not employed at the same location, and is a stranger, so many game designers do much of their work alone.

Alternately, if the sentence's writer really meant more than one person, "everybody" will need to be changed, along with the other quantity signals, to "The employees have different job descriptions, are not employed at the same location, and are strangers, so many game designers do much of their work alone.

The last sample in this section has a mixed signal of quantity that may be the easiest of all to see:

The Product Development Department shortened the list of potentials games for consideration.

This is a case of one "s" too many, the solution being "The Product Development Department shortened the list of potential games for consideration." In a way this is like mixed signals of quantity in one of the sample sentences, "I agree that one can be a genius in one's owns head" and "Some people say that video games rots the brain," (both discussed and solved earlier in this chapter).

Samples of Questions, Directions, and Exclamations

The sample sentences above have one thing in common. Each one is a statement, the most common kind of sentence. Questions, directives (sometimes called "commands"), and exclamations of shock or surprise can also have mixed quantity signals. These first four samples are questions.

Questions

The question, "how many do you mean?" shouldn't be asked in this case, since "which ones can you count?" would be closer to the root of the problem in this first sample question:

How much do your plannings really work out your gaming moves and produce good results?

Like "public transportation" in the Samples of Expanded Sentences and Solutions, above, "plannings" is another "non-countable" word whose quantity is always one. Since "do" would need also to signal a different quantity to reflect that fact, the solution would read like this: "How much does your planning really work out your gaming moves and produce good results?"

This next one's quantity signal is mixed because the number of persons is unclear:

Doesn't video gaming require gamer to make split-second decisions?

Does the sentence's writer mean more than one particular gamer? If that was the intended quantity, the solution is "Doesn't video gaming require gamer_s_ to make split-second decisions?" Otherwise, if just one gamer was the intention, this would read, "Doesn't video gaming require _a_ gamer to make split-second decisions?" Take note of the fact that a negative word in a question like this one means a writer has to drop an "s" and use "requir_e_" and not "requir_es_."

The next sample sentence is a question that runs into trouble for two reasons that affect each other:

Should you use the answers key in the back of the book, or will you learn more if you don't look at them?

As is the case with "I agree that one can be a genius in one's owns head" in Samples of Basic Sentences and Solutions above, "answers" cannot show quantity because it just describes "key," so it is unable to signal quantity, at least by itself. Later in the sentence, "them," a word that does signal quantity, may be signaling the right quantity only if the quantity of both "answer" and "key" are clear: "Should you use the answe_r_ key in the back of the book, or will you learn more if you don't look at _it_?" Otherwise, the solution would be, "Should you use the answe_r_ key_s_ in the back of the book, or will you learn more if you don't look at _them_?"

Also like "public transportation," this fourth question runs into trouble because of a non-countable word whose quantity signal is always one:

Wouldn't the exercises in your homeworks get done faster if you didn't check your phone every five minutes?

The solution is also like the solution to "public transportation_s_": "Wouldn't the exercises in your homewor_k_ get done faster if you didn't check your phone every five minutes?"

Directions

These next four samples are simply the four questions above, taken and re-phrased as commands or directives below:

Do your plannings to work out your gaming moves to produce really good results.

This one has the same solution that it has in its question version: "Do your planning to work out your gaming moves to produce really good results."

This next direction has a different quantity mix-up than it did in its question form, however:

Make split-seconds decisions in your video gaming.

This is different than the question form ("Doesn't video gaming require gamer to make split-second decisions?"). The reason is that many sets of directions are written for the reader to follow. This time, the cause of the mixed signal of quantity is one too many letter "s": "Make split-seconds decisions in your video gaming." The solution is simple: "Make split-second decisions in your video gaming."

This next one has a similar mixed quantity, one exactly like it did in question form above:

Turn off your cell phone or smartphone and avoid all other distractions, so you will complete the exercises in your homeworks quickly.

Again, re-writing one of the above questions as a directive for the reader to follow changes the tone and relation to the reader a little, but the solution is the same. Look back to its question form to see its solution.

This fourth sample also re-phrases the question into a directive, which likewise reads as a task for the reader to perform:

Use the answers in the back of the book, but will you learn more if you don't look at it before you finish.

This time, there is a clear quantity signal at the start of the sentence with "answers," but the signal gets mixed with "it." The solution depends on whether there is in fact more than one answer or not: "Use the answers in the back of the book, but will you learn more if you don't look at them before you finish" (or) "Use the answer in the back of the book, but will you learn more if you don't look at it before you finish."

Exclamations

These last two samples are phrased as exclamations that express shock or surprise:

All this foodstuffs will spoil!

Like "surroundings," this is another case of a word that is always more than one since "foodstuffs" is not countable: All these foodstuffs will spoil!

This last one is yet one more case of one "s" too many:

Video games sharpens the mind!

Either the one who wrote this exclamation was just excited about one game, as in "A video game sharpens," or many games, as in "Video games sharpen the mind!"

2. Finding Solutions through Dialog with a Reader

This middle part of this chapter demonstrates how a writer can access a valuable resource, namely a reader. Someone doesn't need to have a degree in English to play the role of the reader. Any person with a high level of English speaking, reading, and writing skills who honestly wants to help can serve as a reader of a student's sentences. The reader's task here is to look for a mixed signal of meaning, quantity in this case, and bring it to the writer's attention when one appears. Starting with a question helps a writer better focus on the sentence and recall what he or she meant. Upon seeing a mixed signal of quantity in a sentence, a reader might very well ask,

"Do you mean one or more than one?"

Writer: More than one? Which sentence do you mean?

Reader: "Some people say that either video games or television rot the brain."

Writer: It's wrong, then?

Reader: It isn't usually a mixed signal of quantity since "video games <u>rot</u> the brain," but this is an unusual case since "television" comes along second and is closest to the next word that needs a quantity signal.

Writer: So it's "either video games or television rot<u>s</u> the brain"? That sounds so wrong.

Reader: It does sound strange, but "television" after "or" makes it just one thing—right next to "rot<u>s</u>."

Writer: Okay, so "Some people say that either video games or television rot<u>s</u> the brain," not "<u>rot</u> the brain," right?

Reader: Right, but only because of the "or" and the quantity of "television." Most multiple quantities get signaled as multiple. Let's see. Here's a typical one in the same paragraph: "For example playing video games tend to be addictive, and many gaming situations may tempt the player to copy the behavior of what they are watching."

Writer: I'm sorry, but I don't see anything that doesn't sound right.

Reader: It does seem okay at a glance, but "playing" is one activity, even if you mean "continuous playing," so "tend" sends a mixed signal of quantity.

Writer: What should it be then?

Reader: Think about the sentence we looked at a minute ago, the one that needed "rots" in place of "rot." What if you actually meant only video games but not television?

Writer: Then "rot" would have been okay.

Reader: Yes, and if "playing" is just one activity?"

Writer: Oh, I get it. It's "tends" in this case, so "playing video games tends to be addictive."

Reader: Good, how about a "player" as "they"? How many do you mean?

Writer: Oh, that was a typo. I meant players in general, so "For example playing video games tends to be addictive, and many gaming situations may tempt the players to copy the behavior of what they are watching," yes?

Reader: You're starting to get it. Here's one more in the next paragraph. "Video games teaches us about triumph over adversity." It's the same kind of mixed signal as the first one.

Writer: Ah! "Video games teach us about triumph over adversity."

Reader: You've got it! Want to try one more to see if you have signaling quantity under control now?

Writer: Sure, this one in the next paragraph seems a little off but not in the same way as the last two. "The software designers are all from a different background." More than one designer means more than one background, so the quantity signal should be "all from different backgrounds."

Reader: Nice job! Oh, there's an alternate way to clear up the quantity. It could go "The software designers are each from a different background."

Writer: True, I could also say, "Each software designer is from a different background," but I think I'll go with "all from different backgrounds."

Reader: That works. Keep up the good work.

Writer: I will, and thanks.

Get ready to have a dialog of your own with a reader if your writing contains mixed signals of quantity. Use this dialog as a model, especially in regard to how both the reader and writer ask questions—the reader to draw the writer's attention to a mixed signal of quantity, and the writer to get additional feedback from the reader.

3. Microlearning Tips for Using what a Reader Has Seen

- When you need to get a reader's response to quantity signals in your own sentences, use that as the next step in developing a sharper eye for seeing them.
- During and after you and a reader sit down together, compare your mixed signals of quantity with your other sentences.
- It's pretty unlikely that you mixed up every single quantity signal in a piece of writing, especially if you wrote a paragraph or more. Look at how some of your sentences did in fact signal quantity correctly by using the correct words or words' endings to express how you meant singular (one) or plural (two or more).
- Use those instances of correctness to guide you in clearly signaling quantity more consistently. For instance, if you forgot a quantity signal like "the" (or put it where you didn't need it), where did you have it in the right place? Was it in front of a clearly "count-able" word? If you had a few mixed signals of quantity because you didn't add an "s" to a word, take a look at where you did, and see if the neighboring words in each case are different, and how early or late in the sentence the mixed signal of quantity appears.
- If you have begun to see some differences between where you mixed a signal of quantity and where you didn't, use a pen or a highlighter on that piece of writing to write some reminders to look at later.

4. Test Yourself

Which sentences in the sample paragraphs below have mixed signals of quantity, and why? Once you find a quantity mix-up, see if you can come up with possible solutions, based on what is likely about the writer's intended meaning.

A Big Night for Pork

Someone left their lights on in the supermarket parking lot. Meanwhile, all hell was breaking loose inside because the annual Porkathon was in full swing, with each shopper filling up their cart with pork roasts, pork chops, pork sausages, and other cuts of succulent pig meat. On a night like that, one could hardly blamed for not being able to restrain themselves. There's many pictures to every story, so picture one group of petulant pork lovers filling up eight carts each with the 16 lbs. they were allowed under the terms of the sale. It's not easy to blame them, considering how good lean pork would be good for their healths. They even tried to cut into the checkout line, but a calm, self-assured checkers put that gang of greasemongers in their place.

The Saints of Quantity

The Highway Patrol pulled us over outside of San Juan Capistrano (named for the patron saint of judges), just south of Los Angeles. After officer collected ID's and ran warrant check on everyone, he looked inside and saw that something didn't look quite right.

"You guys aren't really part of a church, are you?"

"Uh no, we're moving up to Sonoma," I said.

"Well, you don't have commercial plates, so you can't transports personal effects."

"We don't want to break the law, but here we are, and these are all the transportations we have right now. What can we do?"

The cop looked back down the road for a second and then at the bus. "The only way you can carry all these stuffs in a vehicle of this type without commercial license plates is if it is a motor home. I'll tell you what, put a sign in the back window saying that these is a house vehicle, and I won't have to cite you."

We thanked him, and as he drove off, I took the cardboard backing out of framed poster that somebody had packed between their dresser and a chest of drawer, and made a sign. I used the edge of a mattresses to brace the "House Vehicle" sign so it would face out of the back window. I had made words large and the back window were about a foot above the motto the previous owner, a church, had painted on back of the bus. Anyone driving behind us saw this:

We had no further trouble from the law after that and started to make pretty good time, going up US 101 through Santa Barbara (named for the patron saint of mathematicians), past Santa Maria (news dealer), and San Luis Obispo (for the patron saint of Colombians).Two days, fifty gallons of gas, and half a cases of brake fluid later, we made it to our new home, a farmhouse in Sonoma County, an hour north of San Francisco (the patron saint of zoos), and 30 minutes west of Santa Rosa (the saints for people ridiculed for their piety).

After making no headway in meeting the neighbors, it seemed the simplest way to avoid a bad cases of social leprosy might just be painting the bus. I got a gallon of flat white house paint and painted the back and then went along the driver's side, where it said "PACIFIC BEACH CHURCH OF THE NAZARENE" in five-inch high black capital letters. I painted over five words and left "THE" just for the hell of it. As for the neighbors, everyone changed his or her impression of us after that.

See the answer key to each self-test in appendix three in the back of this book as "A Big Night for Pork" and "The Saints of Quantity." Try to resist the temptation to go there before you finish here. Surprise is a good learning experience.

The Problem of Accurately Telling Time

Take a minute to think about the various ways we talk about time. We can take a simple statement like, "She wrote a letter to her employer," and right away see it as something that happened in the past. The person who wrote it opted to put the situation in a kind of "simple past," but could have chosen the letter to both start and stop in the past by writing, "She <u>had written</u> a letter to her employer" or "She <u>was writing</u> a letter to her employer." The first of these two options adds a bit of suspense by implying that something occurred after she started writing. The sentence's writer seems to suggest something is important about the fact that she "had written" it, as if to prepare a reader for what happened next. The other option implies that something interrupted her; by saying "she was writing," it also adds a little suspense. "She <u>would have written</u> a letter to her employer" adds so much suspense that it can barely stand alone as a sentence, so it's often followed by "but" or "if" in the same sentence: "She would have written a letter to her employer, <u>but</u> there was a blackout"; "She would have written a letter to her employer <u>if</u> she had not just been laid off." Take notice how this paragraph had five other time signals using either the past or the present. Add the future to the kind of mystery that can only be solved when time signals need clearing up, and it is clear there will be plenty to consider in this chapter.

You need to clearly signal what point in time you mean by signaling with words or phrases that "tell time" in your sentence. This chapter will show what some of those are and show how mixed signals of time typically happen, what the solutions look like, how a reader can aid a writer in seeing mixed time signals, and how you can develop an eye for seeing and repairing them. Take a few minutes to preview this chapter's four sections, which you will see **numbered and titled in bold**.

1. What Can Happen when a Time Signal Gets Mixed in a Sentence

Mixed time signals can happen in any kind of sentence, ranging from basic or relatively simple sentences to ones that read as expanded versions of basic sentences. When a writer didn't clearly signal time, the sentence doesn't read well.

Samples of Basic Sentences and Solutions

One of the most common ways time gets mixed is a good place to start:

TV shows have became an important influence.

This is a mix of time signals because "became" signals the past in the most simple way, as in as in "TV shows <u>became</u> an important influence," yet the writer could have meant the present: "TV shows <u>have become</u> an important influence." The writer will need to make clear which time he or she meant, the past or present. Alternately, by adding "have," the person who wrote the sentence may have intended to signal the past in a continuous way, as in "TV shows <u>have been becoming</u> an important influence." This means either that the shows had this effect in the past, all the way up to the present, or that they had this effect and will continue to have it until some point in the future. Since any of these three possible solutions changes the actual time signal, a writer would need to hear that a reader needed to know for certain.

A sentence could consistently signal a specific time and still be confusing, though:

There is a lot of violence involve in today's popular TV shows.

It signals the present, but the confusing part is *how* it signals the present. What is happening is that "involve" is the "root" form of the word, so it signals no time at all. The complete signal for the present time would be "There is a lot of violence involved in today's popular TV shows" since "is" signals the present as in "violence is involved" and changing the word's ending adds the signal of the violence being in the present.

This next one is a classic:

Being an immigrant means having had to cling tenaciously to optimism.

This is an all-to-common mixed time signal, with "means," as a simple signal of the present, mixed with "having had to cling," signaling an action that happened for a period of time in the past. If the sentence's writer did not intend the action to start and then stop in the past, he or she could signal just the continuous past, by adding the simple past of "meant" and deleting "had": "Being an immigrant meant clinging tenaciously to optimism." Since "being" by itself is continuous for any time (past, present, or future), the sentence could also signal the continuous present with a little help from "means" and "having": "Being an immigrant means having to cling tenaciously to optimism."

While writers can signal the future in simple and continuous ways, sometimes an action signaled in the future may or may not be a sure thing:

By this time next week, his living room would have been decorated in the style 1950s America.

The sentence's lead-in signals a week into the future, yet take note that "would have been" could signal that something possible, the decorating, was underway before next week, or that the decoration was being postponed. We might want to confirm with the person who wrote the sentence that a possibility about the future is the whole idea here. Depending on the certainty or possibility about the intended time, the solution could be "By this time next week, his living room <u>will be</u> decorated in the style 1950s America," or if the outcome actually is just a possibility, "By this time next week, his living room <u>could be</u> decorated in the style 1950s America."

Samples of Expanded Sentences and Solutions

Expanding a basic sentence adds to what it describes, but it still needs to clearly signal what point in time the writer meant. This first expanded sentence resembles the sample above since "would have been" plays a part. In this case, the sample contains a switch that makes the writer's intended time signal much harder to guess:

There would have been two types of television he will have mentioned by the end of his presentation, dramatic shows and reality shows.

Somehow putting "would have been" in the first part of the sentence apparently makes all the difference (compared to the fourth basic sentence sample) because the time signal seems all the more confusing here, with "will have mentioned" signaling the future and "would have been" signaling the possible past of both now and the future. We end up wondering what changed his plans in the middle of the sentence. The sentence's writer may have meant "There <u>will be</u> two types of television he will have mentioned by the end of his presentation, dramatic shows and reality shows," but just to be sure, we should ask.

This next one has a very obvious time mix-up:

It will be considered cheating if someone had been copying a classmate's paper.

In this case, we would only need to ask the person who wrote the sentence which time was intended, the future, signaled at the beginning of the sentence, or the past, signaled by "had been copying." It has to be one or the other: the future, as in "It will be considered cheating if someone <u>will have been copying</u> a classmate's paper"; or the possible past, as in "It <u>would have been</u> considered cheating if someone had been copying a classmate's paper." Additional information about the specific time could clear this up as well: "It will be considered cheating if someone had been copying a classmate's paper <u>during</u> the exam."

The third sample contains a common error many writers make when they speak of something that occurred in the past that relates to something else that had happened earlier in the past:

That particular reality show participant had not been doing so well, but now she advanced ahead of the others last week.

Of course a reader would have to ask the writer of this sentence whether the show's participant had advanced in the past or "now," the immediate present, meaning the time when the sentence was written. If the sentence's writer had truly meant two different occurrences, one after the other, but both in the past, the intended time signal would straighten out as "That particular reality show participant had not been doing so well, but <u>then</u> she advanced ahead of the others last week."

The time signals in this fourth sample seem all over the place:

Even though many people will question this, critical thinking is going to occur when a viewer had been keeping track of so many characters.

If the writer meant the present in a continuous way, his or her solution would be "Even though many people <u>question</u> this, critical thinking is going to occur when a viewer <u>is keeping</u> track of so many characters." Take note of the fact that even just the main part of the sentence (" . . . critical thinking <u>is going</u> to occur when a viewer <u>is keeping</u> track of so many characters") could signal the continuous present while the first part could signal a reaction in the future, with "Even though many people <u>will question</u> this . . ."

Samples of Questions, Directions, and Exclamations

Whether a basic sentence or an expanded one, each of the previous sample sentences is a statement, the most common type of sentence. Mixed signals of time in questions, directions (sometimes in the form of a command), and exclamations, can all be especially confusing, though.

Questions

These first four samples are questions. This first sample question seems to give the reader a mystery to solve:

Since demand for services is high and each worker is kept busy, was any conversing allowed?

To ask a follow-up question, why was the conversing between workers only an issue in the past? The rest of the question signals the present and could also mean the continuous present, so the writer will need to clarify whether the conversations of the workers were only a matter of curiosity about the past or still worth asking about in regard to the present. If the concern is the present, the solution is "Since demand for services is high and each worker is kept busy, is any conversing allowed?" If the past is in fact the matter at hand, the solution is "Since demand for services was high and each worker was kept busy, was any conversing allowed?"

This one below is drawn from one of the previous samples of statement-type sentences, and it shows how just a small change in the sequence of words can turn a statement into a question:

Will it be considered cheating if someone had been copying a classmate's paper?

Even though the words' sequence is different, with the information on hand here, the problem remains the same, namely the first part of the sentence signaling the future and the second part signaling that the copying had started and apparently been completed before some time in the future.

This next one also comes from the samples of statement sentences above. The split in time signals is different here, though:

How is it possible that particular reality show participant who had not been doing so well has now advance ahead of the others last week?

This time, the signal of the sentence's present time, "how is it possible," works fine in asking about the past situation of someone "who had not been doing" well, but it stops cold at "has now advance." Like the statement form of the question, a writer would need to clarify whether the reality show's participant had advanced in the past at some point ("had then advanced ahead of the others") or, alternately has just advanced: "How is it possible that particular reality show participant who had not been doing so well has now advanced ahead of the others last week?" Make a note of how the –ed in "advanced can express the present or the past with "has now advanced" or "had then advanced."

This last question, also drawn from previous samples, leaves one more question to answer than it asks:

Can his living room have been decorated in the style 1950s America by this time next week?

It's fair to ask if the writer is asking about a future possibility, as in "Will his living room be decorated in the style 1950s America by this time next week?" Alternately, the intention might have been to ask about possibility of the decorating being completed at a certain time future: "Will his living room have been decorated in the style 1950s America by this time next week?"

Directions

Taking a question from up above and changing some of the words' sequence rephrases it as a directive for the reader to follow. The solution to each is similar to its statement form up above. In each case, the solution below mirrors the solution to its question form above.

For example, this one is almost identical to its question form above:

Since demand for services is high and each worker is kept busy, no conversing was allowed.

The confusion is still over what time the writer meant, but this tells the reader that not talking was the rule at some point in time. If that time is right now, when the reader first sees this, the solution is "Since demand for services is high and each worker is kept busy, no conversing is allowed." If the ban on talking is from the time the reader sees this and also in the future, the solution is "Since demand for services is high and each worker must be kept busy, no conversing will be allowed." In both of these cases, even if the time signaled in each solution is slightly different, the directive asks for the same response that will begin at the same time and continue.

Even directives like "No dogs are allowed on the beach" are actually for the person reading them (since dogs cannot read). This next one takes a question that asked a reader about cheating and turns it into a command:

It will be considered cheating if someone had been copying a classmate's paper.

In order for a reader to avoid copying as directed, he or she might need to know whether or not the writer meant the future: "It will be considered cheating if someone copies a classmate's paper." Even putting the time signals clearly in the past may get the point across that the rule is still in effect: "It has been considered cheating if someone has been copying a classmate's paper."

Speaking of rules, some apply to competitions:

A particular reality show participant who had not been doing so well can now advance ahead of the others last week.

Naturally the person who wrote this rule will have to answer a few questions, especially about whether "not doing so well" has to start and stop in the past (with "had not been"), so if the rule still applies, "A particular reality show participant who had not been doing so well can <u>later</u> advance ahead of the others <u>the</u> <u>following</u> week." If the rule is an old one that is no longer in effect, the writer would have to clear that up for readers by saying, "A particular reality show participant who had not been doing so well <u>could later</u> advance ahead of the others <u>a</u> <u>week later</u>.

This last one gets at the difference between a question and a directive:

The living room must have been decorated in the style 1950s America by this time next week.

A reader might wonder if the writer knew that something in the past had prevented the completion of the decorating job. If the writer actually intended to signal the job to be completed in one week's time, the signal should clearly indicate it: "The living room <u>will have to be</u> decorated in the style 1950s America by this time next week." Even expressing it as a clear possibility would do that:" The living room <u>should be</u> decorated in the style 1950s America by this time next week."

Exclamations

These last two samples are phrased as exclamations that express shock or surprise:

The first version of this was back in Samples of Expanded Sentences and Solutions, as "It will be considered cheating if someone had been copying a classmate's paper." Re-phrasing it to show surprise makes it shorter:

You will be cheating when you had been copying a classmate's paper!

The time signals still need straightening out, though. Whoever would have written this probably didn't necessarily mean you specifically, a problem we'll get to in the next chapter, but the writer still needs to be asked whether the cheating starts in the future even though it seemed to have started in the past. The writer would need to confirm which time he or she meant, but the obvious solution could be the present as well as the future: "You <u>are cheating</u> <u>when you copy</u> a classmate's paper!" or

"You will be cheating <u>when you copy</u> a classmate's paper!" In both of these cases, "<u>when you copy</u>" fits the other time signal in the sentence. It does seem like an accusation though, so if the writer wanted to tone it down a little, putting it in terms of a possibility would be better: "You <u>would</u> be cheating <u>if you copy</u> a classmate's paper!

See the way this one is phrased as a direction, above, then note how some details get left out:

His living room had been decorated in the style 1950s America!

Sometimes a sentence by itself clearly signals time. The original "statement" version earlier in this chapter had more time signals, which needed un-mixing: "By this time next week, his living room would have been decorated in the style 1950s America." In contrast, the exclamation version is shorter, without the part about planning ("By this time next week"). That part is left out here to increase the sense of surprise. Still, the time signal in this version is clear if, and only if, the writer meant the decorating had already been started and completed in the past.

2. Finding Solutions through Dialog with a Reader

This section of the chapter demonstrates how a writer can make use of a valuable resource, namely a reader. Someone who doesn't know all of the grammatical rules can still serve as a reader. In fact, any proficient English speaker who has excellent reading and writing skills and is willing to help can serve as a reader. The reader's task here is to look for mixed time signals, and bring it to the writer's attention any time one appears. The best starting point might be for the reader to ask a question to focus on a particular sentence and prompt the writer to recall what he or she meant. Upon seeing a mixed time signal in a sentence, a reader might very well ask,

"When do you mean?"

Writer: Do you mean my thesis, "Even though many people will question this, critical thinking is going to occur when a viewer had been keeping track of so many characters"?

Reader: Yes, it works fine as a thesis, though there is some the confusion over whether you mean the viewer stopped keeping track of the characters or that the viewer had to do that all the way through the show.

Writer: I get it. It needs to be clear that a viewer, any viewer, has to keep doing that in order to keep up with what's happening. Would "critical thinking is going to occur when a viewer <u>has to be keeping</u> track of so many characters" make the time clearer?

Reader: Yes it would. By the way, economizing the time signal to "<u>is keeping</u> track" will work just as well for meaning the viewer's critical thinking for the whole show, from beginning to end.

Writer: Thanks, I'll use that. Are there any more mixed time signals in my essay?

Reader: I see just two more. Do you see the next sentence with "had been" in it?

Writer: You mean "That particular reality show participant had not been doing so well, but now she advanced ahead of the others last week"?

Reader: Yes, it's that one. Do you mean that the person on the show advanced not now, today, but last week on the show?

Writer: That's right, last week.

Reader: So if it was in the past, of course, it can't be "now" at the same time.

Writer: Oh, duh! How about "That particular reality show participant had not been doing so well, but <u>then</u> she advanced ahead of the others last week"?

Reader: Yes, the time signal is clearer from one point in the past to another. See if you can locate the final mixed time signal. I'll give you a hint: it's in the same paragraph.

Writer: Got it! It's just two sentences later: "Will his living room have been decorated in the style 1950s America by this time next week?" This is the challenge part of the show, so I'll need an alternative to "had been" that puts it in that future episode of the show?

Reader: Yes.

Writer: Okay, but what if I just trim it down to "<u>Will</u> his living room <u>be decorated</u> in the style 1950s America by this time next week?"

Reader: Nice job!

3. Microlearning Tips for Using what a Reader Has Seen

- As a necessary step toward improvement, you need to get a reader's response to time signals in your own sentences. This is the next step in developing a sharper eye for seeing mixed time signals in your sentences, so when you and a reader sit down together, compare your mixed signals with your other sentences. Mark the mixed time signals.
- You did not mix every single time signal in every sentence you wrote, especially if you wrote a paragraph or more. Look at how some of your sentences did in fact signal time correctly by using the correct words or words' endings to express how you meant a particular point in time. Mark as many faultless time signals as you can find, and mark them differently from how you marked any mixed time signals you and your reader found and changed.
- Compare those time signals in your sentences, and use them to guide you in clearly signaling time more consistently. For instance, if you forgot a time signal like "had been" (or put it where you didn't need it) in one sentence, where did you have it in the right

place? Was it in a sentence where something started in the past and then was completed later in the past? If you had a few mixed time signals because you didn't show an action occurring from the past, but also continuing into the present and onward to the future, take a look at where you did, and see if the neighboring time signals are different, and how early or late in the sentence the mixed time signal appears.

4. Test Yourself

Which sentences in the sample paragraph below have mixed signals of time and why? Once you find a mixed-up time signal, see if you can come up with possible solutions based on what is likely about the writer's intended meaning.

Signaling Time in a News Commentary

Refer to this grid of time signals to figure out the correct ones for the paragraph below. "Take" and "leave," the two words used in their root forms, are not examples of how every word would look with a time signal since some words' spelling will change as their time signals change.

The Time Grid				
Time signal	Root	Example phrase	Root	Example phrase
present simple	take	we/you/they take	leave	we/you/they leave
present continuing		— are taking		— are leaving
present completed		— have taken		— have left
present continuing then completed (or to be completed)		— have been taking		— have been leaving
present possible		— may/might/ would/should/ could/can take		— may/might/ would/should/ could/can leave
present possible and continuing		— may/might/ would/should/ could/can be taking		— may/might/ would/should/ could/can be leaving
past simple	take	we/you/they took	leave	we/you/they left
past continuing		— have been taking		— have been leaving

past completed		— had taken		— had left
past continuing then completed		— had been taking		— had been leaving
past completed in the past		— having had taken		having had left
past possible		— may/might/ would must/ should/could have taken		— may/might/ must would/ should/could have left
past possible and continuing		— may/might/ would /should/ could have been taking		— may/might would/should/ could have been leaving
future simple	take	we/you/they will take	leave	we/you/they will leave
future continuing		— will be taking		— will be leaving
future completed		— will have taken		— will have left
future continuing then completed (or to be completed		— will have been taking		— will have been leaving
future possible		— may/might/ would /should/ could have taken		— may/might/ would/should/ could have left
future possible and continuing		— may/might/ would /should/ could be taking		— may/might/ would/should/ could be leaving

All of the spots with time signals in the paragraph below have the root word in parentheses instead of the correct time signal. Your task is to refer to this grid and then choose the right time signals below based on the examples in the grid. Not all of root forms in the paragraph are covered by the grid, nor will every single one of the time signals in the grid have a place in the paragraph. Also, not all of the words in parentheses below will need to be changed, but many will need changing.

The News Commentary

What (be) it really like at Galileo's trial or Lincoln's *Gettysburg Address?* A lot of history's great events in the past (take) place a long time ago, but even relatively recent events (illustrate) the problem of getting the complete picture of what it (be) like to (be) there. When we (see) a television news story about Bruce Springsteen's duet with Paul McCartney onstage at the Live Nation concert in London's Hyde Park just a few nights ago, we only (get) the images and sound that the video and audio equipment (capture) and the words of news reporters who may (be) or may not (be) there. If we manage to find an audience member who (witness) the event in person, we might ask if the concert (be) really loud enough to generate the noise complaints from residents living across the street at the far end of the park, which (be) the source of complaints that the authorities (use) in setting the strict curfew that prematurely (end) the performance. Even if that person could (hear) the sound as it (bounce) off of the buildings, we (be)(leave) to rely on someone else's personal impression of how it (feel). Multiply that by dozens of journalists and television crews, a handful of newspaper photographers, hundreds of people who (take) amateur videos of the concert, and thousands of the people who (listen) and (watch) from various parts of the concert area in the park, we would still (be) (leave) with an incomplete impression of what (happen) that night. We never (get) a 100% complete impression because some small but important detail (escape) the eyes and ears of those who (witness) the event, (do) not (get) (report) at all or, if it (have) (witness), (get) (leave) out as not important enough to report. That (make) us pause and wonder whether or not we (assume) that people a century from now (get) an accurate impression of a major event in our own time.

See "Time to Check" in the appendix three in the back of this book for the answer key to this self-test. Try to resist the temptation to go there before you finish here. You will make better use of your time that way.

Identity

The "You *Who*" Problem

Like quantity signals, identity signals get mixed because everyday casual usage can get confusing when it appears on the page. Saying "you" to someone in a conversation, as in "you never want to buy a car in its first model year" can often mean anybody rather the person to whom you are speaking. That is easily understood by you and your listener because at the start of the conversation, your reference to a situation that in fact applies to neither of you also combines with other cues that prevent confusion. On the page, making that kind of reference to a supposed "you" seems unclear, and your reader may be a complete stranger who wonders who that "you" in your sentence actually means.

Notice that I have been addressing you, the reader, and only the context, the fact that you have picked up this book and understand its purpose, makes it possible to address you directly, but only so long as the topic is your own writing. So outside of this topic, if I were to say "you probably first heard about graffiti when you attended a public high school," you might wonder why I was so reckless about jumping to such a conclusion about your background. In sum, when you write a sentence that references "you" "your" or "yourself," it may confuse a reader about who you actually mean. Even if it's impractical to name names, there are many other words for signaling identity: "someone," "somebody," "people," "anybody," "anyone," "an individual," "individuals," and so on.

One way or another, a writer will have to signal the identity of the person or persons he or she means. What goes for people likewise goes for things with such identity signals as "that," "it," "which," "this," "those," "these," and "things," but this point will need a little more explaining. This chapter will show how mixed signals of identity typically happen, what the solutions look like, how a reader can aid a writer in seeing mixed identity signals, and how you can develop an eye for seeing and repairing them. Take a few minutes to preview this chapter's four sections, which you will see **numbered and titled in bold**.

1. What Can Happen when the Identity Signal Gets Mixed in a Sentence. "the" vs. "A"

Since so many of the commonly mixed signals of identity come from casual conversation, a couple of commonplace expressions should lead this section.

Samples of Basic Sentences and Solutions

This first one is a sample of what we could call a "who, me?" statement:

You need to choose a major that matters to you.

A reader might wonder, "Are you talking to me?" True, some readers may still be weighing their options when they start college, but many others start college with their major in mind. Even though the sample sentence's writer gives good advice, the use of "you" can distract a reader away from the value of the advice. If you get the opportunity to ask the writer, and the answer is "No, I meant anyone starting college who hasn't already chosen a major," then the solution is simple: "<u>Anyone starting college</u> needs to choose a major <u>that matters to him or her</u>."

In other cases, the source of confusion is not "who" but "what" a writer means:

That is how it goes.

This is a classic case of context and meaning. If "it" clearly makes it easy to identify the intended meaning by checking nearby sentences, the cause-and-effect relation of "that" and "it" is clear. Otherwise, a reader will wonder about what they both mean.

Like the sample above, context is the key. In this case, what "which" identifies needs to be clear before the sentence even begins:

The problem isn't which, but who and where.

For the identity signal to work, the solution has to be in the previous sentence, so in this case, think of the identity signal as needing a pair of sentences:

"<u>Most people walk around looking for the right booth at the campus Job Fair, which is the booth with the 'Now Interviewing' sign</u>. The problem isn't which but who and where."

This fourth one is rich with mixed signals of identity since it has one shown in the first sample:

You should know neither this nor that ever happened.

This one begins with another "who, me?" moment. Instead of asking the sentence's writer that question, a reader might focus on asking about the person or people that "you" actually means. Usually the writer had an anonymous individual or the average person in mind: "<u>Anybody</u> should know neither this nor that ever happened." Like "which" in the previous sample, the identities of what "this" and "that" are signaling need to made clear—in a nearby sentence.

Samples of Expanded Sentences and Solutions

Mixed signals of identity happen often in everyday conversation and show up in people's writing in many kinds of sentences, from relatively basic sentences like the samples above to the expanded ones below. When a writer didn't clearly signal the identity he or she meant, the sentence doesn't read well, and the reader can get distracted by any mixed identity signals. The identity signal in this first expanded sentence suffers for a similar reason that the previous sample does:

Few people know that some dialects are seldom heard, but usually appear on the page and such.

This time "that" causes no confusion for a reader, but he or she would be right to ask "to what does 'such' refer?" It seems to have little to do with dialects or pages, so it's time to ask the writer, "What do you mean?" Suppose for a minute that the writer meant "such" to identify various textual media, like documents, text messages, websites, and video captions. Then the fact that all of these appear on the screen could suggest a kind of shortcut as a solution: "Few people know that some dialects are seldom heard but usually appear on the page and <u>on the screen</u>."

Speaking of screens, this next one puts "you" and TV together:

The problem with watching television is that you only stay in a passive mode and don't develop your critical thinking skills.

The writer may have meant the average person, but putting "you" there increases the chances of the statement being factually incorrect—some people who are critical thinkers will disagree because they will think "you" means them. If the writer actually did mean the average person, the solution is a ready-made one: "The problem with watching television is that the <u>average person</u> only <u>stays</u> in a passive mode and <u>doesn't</u> develop <u>his or her</u> critical thinking skills."

While this one offers good advice, like "You need to choose a major that matters to you," earlier in this section, the advice here may not get taken seriously for the same reason—the "who, me?" issue:

After checking your essay's introduction and thesis and then your paragraphs' organization and support for any of the errors you made on previous essays, you should read your sentences backwards to check your proofreading.

Not all writers may have made errors in organization or support (or *both*, the way the sentence reads). In that case, if the problematic areas of their writing are not in organization and support but proofreading instead, the writers considering this advice could reasonably conclude that the whole sentence doesn't apply to them. If we could ask the sentence's writer anything, the question "What kinds of errors?" comes to mind, and if the answer is something along the lines of any type of errors in any area, he or she might consider using another identity signal and deleting most of the original ones: "After checking <u>the</u> essay's introduction and thesis and then <u>the</u> paragraphs' organization and support for any of the errors <u>made</u> on previous essays, <u>writers</u> should read <u>their</u> sentences backwards to check <u>their</u> proofreading."

The fourth sample of an expanded sentence that has mixed identity signals is this one involving people who may have the same identity throughout the sentence:

One example is "textese," the dialect common to text messaging. "OMG!" you might say in surprise, though he or she may not know (FYI) that textese has been evolving over the last decade or so, and has its origins in "geek-speak," the written dialect that sprouted up in email in the late 1980s and early 1990s.

Naturally, if the writer has "you" saying this, who is the "he or she" who arrives seven words later? If the writer's answer is that "It's the same person, somebody who is surprised," then the solution means an easy fix: One example is "textese," the dialect common to text messaging. 'OMG!' <u>a reader</u> might say in surprise, though he or she may not know (FYI) that textese has been evolving over the last decade or so, and has its origins in "geek-speak," the written dialect that sprouted up in email in the late 1980s and early 1990s."

Samples of Questions, Directions, and Exclamations

Questions

Whether a basic sentence or an expanded one, each of the sample sentences above is a statement, the most common type of sentence. Mixed signals of identity in questions, directions (or commands), and exclamations, are especially confusing, though. These first four samples are questions. This first one is a common saying that many people have heard as either a statement or question:

Isn't it really who you know and not what you know?

Seeing this question on the page changes the context, though. Not every reader's personal connections are more valuable than knowledge. A reader needs to ask the question's author who he or she actually meant. It's likely the writer's answer would lead to a solution something like this: "Isn't it really who <u>one</u> knows and not what <u>he or she</u> knows?"

The next two questions are based on sentences that appear as statements earlier in this section:

Isn't the problem who and where and not which?

Like the statement version of this question, "which" must clearly signal something in the previous sentence:

"<u>Most people walk around looking for the right booth at the campus Job Fair, which is the booth with the 'Now Interviewing' sign</u>. Isn't the problem who and where and not which?"

This question may prompt readers to ask a question of their own:

Why is it so easy to pass yourself off as tech-savvy on social networking sites like *Facebook*, *Linked-In*, or *Zoosk*?

A reader should wonder, "If you don't mean me, who do you mean?" For readers, the writer's answer to this question would make the solution pretty obvious. For the moment, let's assume that the writer answers that "yourself" means any individual who does behave that way: "Why is it so easy to pass <u>oneself</u> off as tech-savvy on social networking sites like *Facebook*, *Linked-In*, or *Zoosk*?"

Like the two samples above, this final question will reappear as a statement-type sentence in this chapter's self-test. The next mixed signal is similar to how "which" gets used in "Isn't the problem who and where and not which?" While the mix-up is similar, the word is different:

Doesn't popular culture make all this rewarding?

One could almost say "this" could mean everything in the world, at least anything people think of as rewarding. To narrow the actual identity down to a clearer signal, a reader would need to first check nearby sentences for a clue as to what "this" identifies. The reader will need to ask the writer, "What does *this* mean, exactly?

Directions

When it comes to signaling identity, directions or commands present a unique problem since the reader is oftentimes being addressed directly, but without the "you" in many cases:

Never eat at a cafe called "Mom's" because with a name like that, the food doesn't need to be all that good.

Although this may be wise advice, bear in mind how easily a directive that implies "you" cannot apply to everyone and therefore risks losing its intended audience. This next one illustrates that truth as well:

Ask for help with the software.

Posted as a helpful directive in a college computer lab, the person who composed it may actually know that some students are already familiar with the available software. Since this actually implies that "(You need to) ask for help with the software" and also "if you need it," a solution would read something like this: "Anyone needing help with the software should ask for it."

This next directive runs into the same trouble and makes it clear it means "you":

Turn off the lights when you leave the laboratory.

While the audience is clear, addressing just anyone runs the risk of unintentionally offending someone, namely a person who is not the first to leave. After checking with the person responsible for composing and posting this directive, the solution could take that possibility into account: "The last person to leave the lab should turn off the lights."

Exclamations

These last two samples are phrased as exclamations that sometimes express shock or surprise. The first one is more like an implied command than an expression of shock or surprise, but it does have a sense of being loud:

Uncle Sam wants you!

This has historically been used for military recruiting. It's possible that not everyone knows that "Uncle Sam" is the nickname for the United States, and it is very possible that not everyone reading this exclamation is eligible for military service.

Here's another well known one:

It's location, location, location!

The question of what exactly "it" needs explaining before anything else can be said about location.

Parts of this last one first appeared earlier in this section in an expanded sentence:

OMG! How you will be surprised to hear that "textese" has been around since the late 1980s and early 1990s!

This may not be true for everyone—every "you" who reads this. The writer needs to be asked who in particular will actually surprised and not all readers or those who already knew about the origins of textese. The solution would depend on the writer's assumptions, but since it all happened to come along as a popular way of communication, the solution could read as "OMG! How those who don't know will be surprised to hear that "textese" has been around since the late 1980s and early 1990s!"

2. Finding Solutions through Dialog with a Reader

Dialog starts a path to improving a piece of writing since it works so well in helping students spot mixed signals of meaning and "un-mix" them. Try to imagine yourself in the role of the writer this time. You have asked a skilled writer to act as your reader because you want to improve your ability to find and fix mixed signals of identity. After taking a couple of minutes to look over what you have written, your reader asks,

"Who do you mean?"

Writer: Do you mean in the first paragraph?

Reader: No, but I'll come back to the first paragraph in a minute. I mean down here in the second paragraph: "That could explain the way people interact on social networking sites like *Facebook*, *Linked-In*, or *Zoosk*, where it is fairly easy to pass yourself off as tech-savvy, even though the software is doing all the complicated stuff." I don't think you mean me personally, but if you mean any reader, do you mean that all people try to pass themselves off that way?

Writer: No, I don't mean you or any other reader, but some people who do that, but not everybody. Others don't want to be deceptive, and even a few actually are tech-savvy.

Reader: Okay, so how could you identify who you mean exactly?

Writer: How about "That could explain the way people interact on social networking sites like *Facebook*, *Linked-In*, or *Zoosk*, where it is fairly easy <u>for some people</u> to pass <u>themselves</u> off as tech-savvy, even though the software is doing all the complicated stuff"?

Reader: Yes, that will identify who you mean. Also, "where it is fairly easy <u>to</u> pass <u>oneself</u> off as tech-savvy" would do the job as well.

Writer: Thanks for the tip, but I think I'll stick with "some people" since that's exactly who I mean. You mentioned coming back to my first paragraph, yes?

Reader: Yes, let me ask you something about signaling identity in this third sentence: "One is how popular culture makes it rewarding, and the other is something we use every day—language." Which *it* do you mean, the class drop rate, the failure rate, or something else?

Writer: Now that I look, that isn't very clear. I mean that people find it rewarding socially—you know, being able to do anything on a computer. I see that I say that in different ways in the next two paragraphs.

Reader: I see you also doing that there, and you'll make the identity here a lot clearer, a good move since it's your thesis. What was that phrase you just used to describe it, "rewarding socially"?

Writer: Right! Maybe this will work better: "One is how popular culture makes it <u>socially rewarding to seem able to do anything on a computer</u>, and the other is something we use every day—language." I left the "it" there, but does the identity signal work?

Reader: Yes it does. Now "it" gets followed by its identity, the meaning: "<u>socially rewarding to seem able to do anything on a computer.</u>"

Writer: Yes, that's definitely better. I have to go to another class now. Can we work on this some more later?

Reader: Sure, no problem. Text me when you want to meet again.

3. Microlearning Tips for Using what a Reader Has Seen

- If you took the bait and put yourself in the writer's shoes in the pervious section, think of how much of a difference there is between what a writer intended to signal and what actually got across to the reader in terms of what meant what—the identity meant with one word standing in for another. Even if you couldn't suspend reality long enough to pretend to be the writer in section 2, "Finding Solutions through Dialog with a Reader," you may have gotten a sense of this gap between a writer's intentions and what a reader understood. Keep that in mind at all times, and you will be doing the kind of thinking that makes for better writing.

- In developing a sharper eye for seeing mixed identity signals in your sentences, compare your mixed signals of identity with your other sentences after you and a reader have sat down together, and see where you signaled the intended meaning of "that," "it," "which," "this," "those," "these," and "things," and so on. Also look at where you found a good alternative to using "you" in a sentence.

- Then look at where the identity of what you meant didn't come across as well as you had intended. Keeping track of the differences between where you succeeded and where you had difficulty is how you begin to quickly improve.

- To make sure you "own" identity signals now, mark those differences between where you mixed an identity signal and where you didn't with a pen or a highlighter.

4. Test Yourself

Check this "mini-essay" for mixed signals of identity by using the footnote for each underlined word. If the identity signal is absent or unclear, you need only say so because making it clear is the writer's job. The footnote of each underlined word is a blank space, where you would say whether the identity signal is clear or not, like this word, for example.[1]

Virtual Identity and Language

I have been doing a lot of thinking about why the class drop rate and the failure rate are noticeably higher in online college classes than they are in the face-to-face versions of the same classes. There are two reasons for this[2]. One is how popular culture makes it[3] rewarding, and the other is something we use every day—language.

While some people freely admit that they are unable to fathom computer software and have little success understanding detailed instructions when they ask for help, many others (maybe the majority) won't admit it[4]. One thing[5] that might explain such quirky behavior by noting how many people in an unfamiliar situation are afraid of seeming dumb, especially in front of strangers. That[6] could explain the way people interact on social networking sites like *Facebook*, *Linked-In*, or *Zoosk*, where it[7] is fairly easy to pass yourself[8] off as tech-savvy, even though the software is doing all the complicated stuff. A prospective student might assume, "Hey, I can use Twitter pretty well, have my own *Facebook* wall with photos, a blog on *Myspace*, and other cool stuff, so what could be so challenging about taking a college course online?"

---

1   *You would write, "The signal is clear here."*
2
3
4
5
6
7
8

In a word, the answer is plenty, mainly because the online course software usually requires them[9] to be more experienced in terms of computer functions and using various kinds of applications. To cite but one example, when I taught a web-based writing course at Washington State University a few years ago, there were more students who had trouble getting help posting their writing on the class site than there were students who had trouble getting help with improving their writing. That is still how it[10] goes. Another way to explain why this[11] happens is popular culture, at least in the sense of how much it assigns a special status to people who seem to be able to quickly do anything on a computer, a smartphone, a tablet, and such[12]. It[13] is just uncool to not keep up with them[14], through web-based social networking, maybe online gaming, and for some, "hooking up" with that special someone. No one wants to be a "web wallflower" these days.

Language always seems to be at the center of this, especially when it[15] comes to popular culture. Most people know what dialects are. Few people know that some dialects are seldom heard, but usually appear on the page and such[16]. These "written dialects" are at the root of the problem. For instance, the written dialect of college educated professionals is standard written English (SWE) and is more formal in its grammar and usage than what most people use in casual communication. One example is "textese," the dialect common to text messaging. "OMG!" you[17] might say in surprise, though he or she may not know (FYI) that textese has been evolving over the last decade or so, and has its origins in "geek-speak," the written dialect that sprouted in email in the late 1980s and early 1990s.

9

10

11

12

13

14

15

16

17

When people have trouble with changing from one written dialect to another, they are either unaware of the correct one for the occasion or lack fluency in the right one. That explains some messages I have been receiving lately that say "i am already in a class but want to switch to yrs." Of course <u>that</u>[18] filled over a month ago (LOL). Though college classes are oftentimes populated by people who are virtually popular online or on the smaller screen of the text message, the medium of communication in college classrooms is still SWE, BTW. One might respond by saying that the jobsite of the nor-too-distant future will require <u>it</u>[19] all. The problem isn't <u>which</u>[20] but who and where.

See the Answer Key to "Identity" in appendix three in the back of this book for some sample responses a reader might write in the footnotes. Try to resist the temptation to go there before you finish here.

18
19
20

How We Locate People and Things

When we write, we are sometimes *at* rest, other times *on* the go, occasionally sitting *down*, and sometimes looking *directly at* the words *on* the page (or screen). As we read, we are *here*, looking *at* this first page *in* a chapter *on* signaling location, *in* this book, and thinking *over* the zigs and zags of signaling location. No wonder this signal gets mixed up!

As the first two sentences of this chapter demonstrate, location doesn't just mean someone or something at rest, either. Location can mean going *toward* or *away from a* position of rest. We all have to clearly signal location one way or another. That could mean a little word, a big one, or a phrase within a sentence. Look for what (or who) moves what direction or what (or who) stays. Consider these location signals for instance:

He gave it <u>to</u> her.

She got it <u>from</u> him.

<u>Between</u> you and me, she got the better deal.

She was <u>near</u> to her car as she slid <u>sideways</u>.

He <u>nearly</u> fell, too.

She is <u>at</u> work now.

If these signals had been mixed, the meaning would be different or just plain difficult to figure out.

When a writer does make an error, a mixed signal of location arrests the reader's attention as easily as a mixed signal of time does. This chapter will show what signaling words signal location and what typically happens when location signals are not clear, what the solutions look like, how a reader can aid a writer in seeing mixed location signals, and how you can develop an eye for seeing and repairing them. Take a few minutes to preview this chapter's four sections, which you will see **numbered and titled in bold**.

1. What Can Happen When a Location Signal Gets Mixed in a Sentence

Location signals can get mixed up in any kind of sentence, in basic sentences or expanded ones. When a writer didn't clearly signal location, something seems strange and hard to follow.

Samples of Basic Sentences and Solutions

This first sample shows how a mixed signal of location can really distort a writer's intended meaning:

I need to know weaknesses I can improve in so I can become a better writer.

If the person who composed this sentence really meant that his or her weaknesses in writing could be made even weaker, the intended meaning is clear. If it turns out that the intended meaning was to work toward fewer or less severe weaknesses, in other words, improved writing, the location signal will need to change: "I need to know weaknesses I can improve <u>on</u> so I can become a better writer."

This next one's missing location signal is pretty comical:

The four of us just hung all night.

Hopefully a quick check with this sentence's writer will verify that four people were not literally hanging from a hook or something. Knowing that, a couple of solutions would not only signal location but clarify what was happening: "The four of us just hung <u>around</u> all night" or more informally, "The four of us just hung <u>out</u> all night."

This next sample comes from a mix of two ways of saying the same thing:

The pizza arrived just on time.

The first way of saying this clearly is "The pizza arrived just <u>in</u> time." The second is "The pizza arrived <u>on</u> time." Either one would work, but what if the writer meant that the pizza "just arrived on time" as if to imply that it <u>just</u> arrived <u>on</u> time, and that was the only good thing about it? A reader would need to ask whether speedy delivery or poor quality was the issue.

This last sample of a basic sentence brings something from regional American speech:

The loud music at the next door neighbor's place close to drove me crazy.

There are actually two mixed signals of location in this sentence. If the sentence's writer meant that he or she was not actually visiting the neighbor, the signal should make the location a bit farther away: "The loud music <u>from</u> the next door neighbor's place close to drove me crazy." The second location signal is clear enough, but it might be helpful to find out if the writer was writing for something that requires a bit more formality, like his or her workplace or a college course. If formality was a consideration, the location signal could be formalized to read, "The loud music <u>from</u> the next door neighbor's place drove me <u>close to</u> crazy."

Samples of Expanded Sentences and Solutions

This first expanded sentence sends two mixed signals of location related to when and where:

In October 6, 2011, I participated in a local economic surveying activity of small businesses in the street where I live.

The sentence's writer would need to clarify two things for a reader. First, a reader will need to know which is more important, only the month or the specific day. If the just the month matters, the location signal "in" would reflect that with "<u>In</u> October, 2011." On the other hand, if the specific date does matter, "<u>On</u> October 6, 2011" would signal that.

For the second location signal, a reader should question whether the writer really meant businesses that are actually situated in the street, like ice cream trucks, mobile auto repair vans, or pedicabs: ". . . I participated in a local economic surveying activity of small businesses <u>in</u> the street where I live." If the businesses in the survey were on or along the sidewalks of the street as store fronts, like shops, markets, and theatres, the location signal would need to be corrected to read, " . . .I participated in a local economic surveying activity of small businesses <u>on</u> the street where I live."

This next one's solution has fewer options:

After we pushed the car to the gas station by the highway, we cooled off at a booth in the Old Prospector Café, one of the two eateries in town.

Once the car gets to the gas station, it is there "at the gas station," so if the sentence's writer meant "<u>in</u> the booth" and not "<u>at</u> the table," his or her decision as to what to change is an easy one. Notice here that size doesn't matter when it comes to "at" or "in." A specific location is often signaled with "in" when the inside or outside does not matter: "After we pushed the car to the gas station by the highway, we cooled off <u>in</u> a booth in the Old Prospector Café, one of the two eateries in town."

Like the basic sentence sample with the four people who "hung," this one is kind of funny:

Even though they put what they hoped to achieve in lists, all of their big dreams went through the window in the form of paper airplanes.

Like the previous extended-sentence sample, this one has one mixed location signal dealing with the action of the people involved. If the sentence's author didn't want to reveal what was on the other side of the window, his or her work on this part of the sentence is done. If the author had a clear direction in mind, "out" would signal that better than "through." Add to that the confusing location signal that involves the act of "listing." If the sentence's writer could confirm that yes, the people were putting things <u>on</u> lists, not using the lists themselves as the actual achievements, the solution would likely be, "Even though they put what they hoped to achieve <u>on</u> lists, all of their big dreams went <u>out</u> the window in the form of paper airplanes."

This last sample in statement form is a playful way of dissecting the old saying, "Tell me no secrets, and I'll tell you no lies," by rephrasing it:

This apparently means that I will not lie to anyone who tells me anything I can freely pass along at others, and I will lie to someone who tells me anything that I cannot pass in to others.

Both of the mixed signals in this one are closely related since the person who composed this sentence could choose to repeat the phrasing in two different parts of the same sentence. Since using "pass" right next to "along" also needs "to," for signaling a specific direction as in "pass <u>along to</u> others," the writer would only need to make the same location signal clear there and then make the same change later: "I will not lie to anyone who tells me anything I can freely pass <u>along to</u> others, and I will lie to someone who tells me anything that I cannot pass <u>along to</u> others." Alternately, "on" would work as well: "I will not lie to anyone who tells me anything I can freely pass <u>on to</u> others, and I will lie to someone who tells me anything that I cannot pass <u>on to</u> others."

Samples of Questions, Directions, and Exclamations

Even though the two sets of the sample sentences above represent the most common type of sentence, the statement, mixed signals of location in the form of questions, directives (or commands), and exclamations of shock or surprise also create confusion about the intended meaning.

Questions

These first four samples are questions. This first one affects the intended meaning in a profound way, as it did in its earlier form as a statement:

Can you help me improve in my weaknesses so I can become a better writer?

The person asking this question very likely wants improved writing rather than improved weaknesses, so the solution will be "Can you help me improve on my weaknesses so I can become a better writer?"

This next question is a hard read:

Don't those people love to argue of how other people argue?

This is an extreme case but one that does happen at times, the kind of mixed-up location signal that just stops a reader cold. The writer could have meant "argue about how other people argue," but some dialog with the writer might also reveal another intended location signal: "argue against how other people argue."

The next one's location signal is mixed in either one or two ways:

Are they still going in and out about the "who," "what," "how," "when," and "where" of people communicating?

As is always the case, a reader and a writer will need to communicate when the intended meaning isn't clear. There are two possible solutions to this one: ". . . still going on and on about . . ." (or) ". . . still going back and forth over the "who," "what," "how," "when," and "where" of people communicating?"

This last question's intended location signal seems altogether absent:

Did you graduate high school in 2002?

This sample comes from casual conversation, maybe because a different version of the same question would need no location signal: "Did your high school graduate you in 2002?" Phrasing it the way it appears above does require the writer to provide a location signal, however: "Did you graduate <u>from</u> high school in 2002?"

Directions

Mixed signals of location in the form of commands or directions for people to follow might actually have some physical consequences if the signals are mixed up. One problem with any confusion about the intended location is that it sometimes affects the tone of the communication, as it could here:

You need to back in right now.

If whoever wrote this meant to give a command for the reader to move a vehicle backwards, both the intended direction and tone seem appropriate, just as "back <u>up</u>" would communicate that kind of movement in a more general way, but imagine a different location being the writer's intention, and notice what happens to the tone: "You need to back <u>away</u> right now." Whoever wrote that sentence had better be avoided. The same goes for someone who really meant "back <u>off</u>."

This third directive is more clearly a piece of good advice, but it may need more clarity:

Define key terms on your argument.

Before making use of this advice, a reader may want the writer to clarify whether those key terms are about the argument's main point, as in "Define key terms <u>of</u> your argument" or terms having to do with the argument's content, as in "Define key terms you use <u>in</u> your argument."

This last one apparently gives the reader no real choice at all:

You have to choose with being told an unpleasant truth or being pleasantly deceived.

If this writer meant that the choice was not between using these but was between choosing one of them to experience, the solution is "between": "You have to choose <u>between</u> being told an unpleasant truth or being pleasantly deceived."

Exclamations

These last two samples are phrased as exclamations that sometimes express shock or surprise. Borrowed from the fourth extended sample sentence and rephrased as an exclamation to express shock or surprise, this first one suggests some kind of magic trick:

I will lie to someone who tells me anything that I cannot pass in to others!

Since passing anything into another person is probably not what this writer meant, some reader-to-writer dialog would help the writer establish the intended location signal, most likely this one: "I will lie to someone who tells me anything that I cannot pass <u>along</u> to others!" Otherwise, "<u>on</u> to others" would serve as a solution.

This exclamation twists the meaning of a common expression of surprise:

You closely gave me a heart attack!

If the person who composed this sentence is okay and in fact did not have a heart attack, a reader would want to ask about what happened. As a very common expression of surprise, the intended location signal would make it read like this: "You <u>almost</u> gave me a heart attack!"

2. Finding Solutions through Dialog with a Reader

Think of yourself looking over the shoulder of someone who a writer has asked for help with signaling location. As you read the end of the first paragraph, you can imagine hearing the reader asking, "Where do you mean?"

Writer: On this line here? "I am telling the truth of lying or lying of telling the truth."

Reader: Yes, in that sentence. Do you mean the act of lying as you are actually typing or the subject of lying? The two are different.

Writer: I see now that I really could be demonstrating lying and saying something about it at the same time.

Reader: So it's "telling the truth about lying" and "lying about telling the truth," yes?

Writer: Yes, like I say down here, toward the end of the paragraph: "A dilemma is typically defined as a difficult problem, a kind of problem that has no easy solution and oftentimes involves a person being forced to make a bad choice between two equally undesirable solutions, like having to choose with being told an unpleasant truth or being pleasantly deceived."

Reader: You have a sharp eye. Notice that "telling the truth about lying" and "lying about telling the truth" have similar phrasing, like "a bad choice between two equally undesirable solutions, like having to choose with being told an unpleasant truth or being pleasantly deceived"?

Writer: I'm not sure what you're asking.

Reader: Notice that the similar phrasing meant repeating "about" in the first one, so what about "between" in the second one?

Writer: Oh, I see. It should repeat the same way: "a bad choice between two equally undesirable solutions, like having to choose between being told an unpleasant truth or being pleasantly deceived," right?

Reader: Yes, that's right. There are two sentences in the paragraph that have to do with the location signal of "on" in one way or another. Let me ask about "I'll lay this puzzle on the doorstep of rhetoricians since this what they might call a 'rhetorical dilemma.'" You don't really mean actually putting a puzzle on somebody's doorstep, right?

Writer: No, I don't. I just mean it in a manner of saying. Would that make it different?

Reader: Yes, it would then be more of a general place, like "at work" or "at the store."

Writer: Oh I get it. So it would be "I'll lay this puzzle <u>at</u> the doorstep of rhetoricians," then?

Reader: Yes, good, how about another use of "on"? Down here you say, "Rhetoricians are people who are fascinated with communication and they communicate that to anyone who cares, going in and out about the 'who,' 'what,' 'how,' 'when,' and 'where' of people communicating."

Writer: I think I see. I would have to be locating this as "going <u>on</u> and <u>on</u>," yes?

Reader: Yes, you've got it. Here's one location mix-up of another kind: "They especially like argument as a type in communication and love to argue of how other people argue."

Writer: Okay, I see how "They especially like argument as a type in communication," should be "They especially like argument as a type <u>of</u> communication," so "love to argue of how other people argue" should be "love to argue <u>about</u> how other people argue." What about this one, "A rhetorical dilemma has to do to the nature of the argument here"? It sounds better than it reads.

Reader: That should tell us something. Remember that parallel phrasing in "telling the truth about lying" and "lying about telling the truth" and "a bad choice between two equally undesirable solutions, like having to choose between being told an unpleasant truth or being pleasantly deceived"?

Writer: Yes, and it looks like a similar parallel phrasing thing here, but it looks strange. What if I make it not parallel, like "A rhetorical dilemma has to do <u>with</u> the nature of the argument here"?

Reader: Yes, that location signal is clearer now. You still have another paragraph to write, don't you?

Writer: Yes, I have one more paragraph to go. Thanks for your help with what I have so far.

3. Microlearning Tips for Using what a Reader Has Seen

- At this point, you need to get a reader's response to location signals in your own sentences. This next necessary step in developing a sharper eye for seeing mixed signals of location in your sentences involves you and a reader sitting down together and later, comparing your mixed signals of location with your other sentences.
- Few writers ever mix up every single location signal in a piece of writing, especially if they wrote more than just a few sentences. Look at how some of your sentences do signal location correctly by using the correct words or phrases to express location. Mark them.
- Use those moments of correctness to create a list in the margins of your piece of writing or down below the last sentence by writing each location signal that got mixed-up and, just to the right of it, the correction you needed for the signal to be clearer for a reader. For instance, did "in" and "on" get mixed, or did "of" and "from"? Did certain other words get mixed in signaling location often enough to reveal a pattern of mixed location signals? Mark any that did.

4. Test Yourself

Which of these underlined words is a mixed signal of location? Just say "yes" or "no" next to each footnote. The footnotes match the numbers next to the location signals.

The Truth about Lying

Everybody lies. I could be lying right now. A reader may now be wondering whether I am telling the truth of[1] lying or lying of[2] telling the truth. Actually I'm doing both. I'll lay this puzzle on[3] the doorstep of rhetoricians since this is what they might call a "rhetorical dilemma." I see that I should quickly define a few terms before I go any further. Rhetoricians are people who are fascinated with communication and they communicate that to anyone who cares, going in[4] and out[5] about the "who," "what," "how," "when," and "where" of people communicating. They especially like argument as a type in[6] communication and love to argue about how other people argue. This may make rhetoricians seem like nervous, suspicious people, and things get worse when a rhetorical dilemma comes along[7]. A dilemma is typically defined as a difficult problem, a kind of problem that has no easy solution and oftentimes involves a person being forced to make a bad choice between[8] two equally undesirable solutions, like having to choose with[9] being told an unpleasant truth or being pleasantly deceived. A rhetorical dilemma has to do to[10] the nature of the argument here.

1
2
3
4
5
6
7
8
9
10

Going back <u>with</u>[11] everybody lying, it's no secret that everybody finds a reason not to tell the truth once <u>on</u>[12] a while. "Everybody" is a term that naturally includes me. To illustrate, let me go to the old saying, "Tell me no secrets, and I'll tell you no lies." In other words, I will not lie to anyone who tells me anything I can freely pass <u>along</u>[13] <u>at</u>[14] others, and I will lie to someone who tells me anything that I cannot pass <u>in</u>[15] <u>to</u>[16] others. That means privacy has true value and lying is one of the ways people protect the bits of information that would become damaging <u>at</u>[17] themselves or others if shared. It follows that I would only lie if the truth about everybody lying is a fact that needs to be kept secret. A good arguer defines the terms <u>in</u>[18] argument. I've just defined three terms, and I'm not lying.

Try to resist the impulse to go straight to the appendices in the back of this book to see the answer key before you have finished here. Right or wrong, you will have a better sense of your own awareness of location that way. The answer key, titled "The Truth About Lying," is in appendix three.

11
12
13
14
15
16
17
18

Transaction

What does one side get from the other?

The "From-One-to-the-Other" Problem

This signal gets mixed up the least, but it does appear on a student's page from time to time. Consider this announcement, for instance: "The registrar requires that a student pays his or her fees by the end of the first week." Since this is directed at only one student reading the announcement at any one time, "pays" seems to express quantity clearly enough. But the student who reads this announcement will instantly become aware that he or she has been directed to do something as part of a transaction with the college's registrar. That situation changes the normal quantity signal to "pay," so "The registrar requires that a student <u>pay</u> his or her fees by the end of the first week." Think of this kind of demand for a specific response as a kind of exchange, where one side gets some action or thing from another.

Some signals of transaction don't show very much in the way of an exchange taking place, but do show some kind of expectation: "With she, they will enjoy fascinating dinner conversation." At a glance, the identity signal may look okay, as with "they will enjoy fascinating dinner conversation," but just like the quantity signal "pays" needing to change to "pay," the implied transaction here requires a slight change of form: "With <u>her</u>, they will enjoy fascinating dinner conversation." Getting the signal right with this type of transaction signal might involve stating the transaction in a different sequence to figure out the solution: "They will enjoy fascinating dinner conversation <u>with her</u>." One quick way to do this is to look for the "actor" in the sentence: "It was I who had it first" (not "It was me"). In sentences where they are used, "I," "he," "she," "they," and "who" are all the actors, while "me," "him," "her," "them," and "whom" are the "receivers," so it also helps to locate the receiver in a sentence:

"He sent the letter to her" (not "she").

"It was me to whom the letter was addressed" (and not "I" and "who" because neither one is the actor here).

"The letter was addressed to Bill and me" (and not "Bill and I").

"Hand it to me, and I will mail it" (which is not necessarily a transaction without "and").

"On him we can depend when it comes to doing the right thing" (and not on "he").

Mixed signals of transaction do not always distort the writer's intended meaning as much as a mixed signal of quantity, identity, or time might, but a reader will often get the feeling that something has gone wrong in the sentence without seeing exactly what it is—a distraction no reader really needs.

This chapter will show what some of those correct words or phrases are as you consider what typically happens when signals of transaction are not clear, what the solutions look like, how a reader can aid a writer in seeing these kinds of mixed signals, and how you can develop an eye for seeing and repairing them. Take a few minutes to preview this chapter's four sections, which you will see **numbered and titled in bold**.

1. What Happens when a Transaction Signal Gets Mixed in a Sentence

When a mixed signal of transaction happens in a sentence, the word can still make sense, but it can make for distracting reading. Whether basic sentences or expanded ones that read as expanded versions of basic sentences, the transaction signal needs to be clear.

Samples of Basic Sentences and Solutions

A good place to start would be one of the most common ways a transaction signal gets mixed:

We believe it is him who removed the contents of the safe.

There are several ways to say what this sentence's writer meant here, and this one communicates quantity and identity clearly. The rough spot is the absence of a transaction between "we" and "him." The path to the solution follows the advice given in this chapter's second paragraph: "One quick way to do this is to look for the 'actor' in the sentence." This sample comes with a twist, though. The actor is "we" creating a new actor out of "him," so "him" becomes "he": "We believe it is <u>he</u> who removed the contents of the safe."

This second sample sentence shows another way a writer can mix the transaction signals:

Between you and I, the professor prefers that Shawn does his reading before he comes to class.

Any writer could fall into the trap of believing that "you" and "I" are the *actors* in this sentence when the professor is focus of the action (with Shawn's reading as the cause of the professor's preference). Putting the actor up front and the receiver after the action, "The professor prefers that Shawn does his reading before he comes to class, between you and I" would show that Shawn is not the only receiver of action, so the writer of the sentence would need to make a few small changes: "Between you and <u>me</u>, the professor prefers that Shawn does his reading before he comes to class." The writer would also need to make one more change because the professor expects some action from Shawn: "Between you and _me_, the professor prefers that Shawn _do_ his reading before he comes to class."

This next one tells the story of an anonymous sign writer expecting some specific action from a reader:

In many a hotel room in the Old West, a sign on the wall requested that a male guest removes his boots before getting into bed.

Like the registrar's requirement in this chapter's first paragraph and the professor's preference above, someone clearly expects some action by someone else: "In many a hotel room in the Old West, a sign on the wall requested that a male guest _remove_ his boots before getting into bed."

This last basic sentence sample may look familiar:

Tell me no secrets; I'll tell you no lies.

Borrowed from the previous chapter, this old saying signals a proposed transaction, but a reader could advise the writer to express it as a transaction in a more straightforward way: "Tell me no secrets, _and_ I'll tell you no lies."

Samples of Expanded Sentences and Solutions

A bit more developed than a basic sentence, this first expanded sentence could easily get by a reader at first glance:

With her approval ratings so low, it is obvious that she does not change her polices and work better with the City Council, she will neither succeed as mayor nor get re-elected to the office.

A reader would probably have a difficult time seeing where the transaction begins in this one. Unlike "Tell me no secrets, and I'll tell you no lies," (and twenty-five words longer), this expanded sentence needs an "if" to signal an outcome as a result of someone's actions: "With her approval ratings so low, it is obvious that _if_ she does not change her polices and work better with the City Council, she will neither succeed as mayor nor get re-elected to the office."

Like the example of the hotel room sign, this next sentence reveals an expectation of action:

Given his tendency to utter loud profanities during the testing period, the staff strongly recommends that the applicant either refrains from swearing or takes the State CPA Exam on another date.

While there are just six more words here than in the basic sentence, "In many a hotel room in the Old West, a sign on the wall requested that a male guest remove his boots before getting into bed," the expected transaction also shows that a word's form needs to change. Should the person who composed the sentence seek a reader's advice, the solution is similar to the "remove his boots" sentence: "Given his tendency to utter loud profanities during the testing period, the staff strongly recommends that the applicant either <u>refrain</u> from swearing or <u>take</u> the State CPA Exam on another date."

This next expanded sentence clearly shows a potential transaction, one that confuses the identity of the "actor" and "receiver":

Every video-gamer should remember that such great skill can come to he or she because whenever a player advances to the game's next level, he or she has acquired experience, assuming that his or her avatar survives the challenges of the earlier levels of the game.

Once again like the sample in this chapter's second paragraph, the sentence's author will need to change the form of the identity signal "he or she" because "to" points the way to the potential "receiver": <u>to him or her</u>. Additionally, the potential meant by "assuming that" points the way to another change a reader should advise the writer to make, namely "survi<u>ve</u>" instead of "survives": "Every video-gamer should remember that such great skill can come to <u>him or her</u> because whenever a player advances to the game's next level, he or she has acquired experience, assuming that his or her avatar survi<u>ve</u> the challenges of the earlier levels of the game."

Here is another "to" situation in this last one:

"Wish you are here" the sender wrote on the back of the postcard that showed Mt. Vesuvius erupting, yet the actual person who the card was addressed remains a mystery because the card was simply addressed to the Philadelphia Police Department.

The writer should solicit a reader's feedback about how using "to" points the way to the identity of potential "receiver," namely "the actual person <u>to whom</u> the card was addressed." At the sentence's beginning, the message "Wish you are here" on the postcard expressed a potential action rather than a certain one, so whoever penned "Wish you are here" will need to signal that potential nature of the transaction as "Wish you <u>were</u> here." (You probably noticed that the postcard's sender also missed an identity signal: "<u>I</u> wish you <u>were</u> here.")

Samples of Questions, Directions, and Exclamations

The sample sentences above share one characteristic. Each one is a statement, the most common kind of sentence. Questions, directives (sometimes called "commands"), and exclamations of shock or surprise can also have mixed signals of transaction. These first three samples are questions.

Questions

It almost goes without saying that a question almost always prompts some kind of interaction, but only some questions need to signal a transaction.

This first question is similar to the last expanded sentence sample in this chapter:

On who can we depend to do the right thing?

Instead of using "to" as the signal for identifying the receiver, the anonymous person "we" are looking to find, the writer of this sentence used "on" because it goes together with the action, as in "depend on." Like the person who wrote "to whom the card was addressed" the solution means a similar change: "On whom we can we depend to do the right thing?" As in a couple of the previous sample sentences, the location signal points the way to the "receiver" in the transaction.

This next one is borrowed from an earlier sample sentence and turned into a question:

Doesn't the management prefer that he climbs into bed not wearing his cowboy boots?

This question version of the sentence shifts the time to the present as it shifts the expected response from "remove" to "climb." Both the reader and writer should note that the time shift doesn't change the form of the word when the expectation of action is expressed this way: "Doesn't the management prefer that he climb into bed not wearing his cowboy boots?"

This last question runs into a signal mix-up one of the expanded sentence samples contains:

Does a rugby player who plays on in spite of minor injuries earn bragging rights for he or she?

Because of the source of the bragging rights is unknown here, the sentence is written so that the rugby player is both the "actor" and the "receiver" in the transaction. The receiver's identity is clear, but the form needs to change: "Does a rugby player who plays on in spite of minor injuries earn bragging rights for himself or herself?"

Directions

These next four samples are commands or directives below and, like questions, prompt a reader to respond. This first directive is one of the questions rephrased:

Keep playing rugby in spite of minor injuries; you will earn bragging rights.

Apparently the person who wrote "you" here meant really any player who reads the sentence will receive something in exchange for the action of playing despite injuries. Still, a reader could wonder whether the bragging rights will just arrive or are being offered, so the transaction just needs to be brought out more: "Keep playing rugby in spite of minor injuries <u>and</u> you will earn bragging rights."

The nature of the transaction seems unclear in this next directive because what could be exchanged may not be clear:

Do not trade information <u>to</u> injury.

A reader may reasonably assume that injury would somehow *receive* information, so the writer will have a small change to make if the intended meaning is that injury is in fact what would get exchanged: "Do not trade information <u>for</u> injury."

This last one runs into the same mixed transaction mix-up that "Wish you <u>were</u> here" solved:

If you was to follow that rule, you will have done something to make the web a better place.

The person who wrote this directive will need to signal the potential transaction by changing the quantity of "was" to "were": "If you <u>were</u> to follow that rule, you will have done something to make the web a better place."

Exclamations

Even though they are expressions of shock or surprise, exclamations sometimes read like basic sentences or other times like directives. Either way, some of them signal a transaction by showing a very strongly worded expectation.

This first one demonstrates that kind of expectation:

We demand that he ceases and desists from dumping engine oil in the storm drains!

Like several of the previous sentence samples in this chapter, the expected transaction shows that a word's form needs to change: "We demand that he cea_se_ and desi_st_ from dumping engine oil in the storm drains!" The writer will need to hear about his or her tendency to choose the right word form to express the potential transaction.

This next exclamation has yet to express a transaction:

Upon return for subscribing to the blog, readers get to join the mayhem!

Right now the sentence's writer is signaling location with "upon return," so a reader should ask if the writer means to signal any kind of transaction. If the readers in the sentence are getting rewarded for subscribing to the blog, the transaction will need signaling: "In return for subscribing to the blog, readers get to join the mayhem!" Of course, "In return" looks like another location signal, but it's a standard way of expressing an exchange.

As a way of signaling intended meaning, this third and final exclamation also needs a transaction in place of a location:

You will avoid willfully inflicting injury toward whoever else is in the game!

The reader of this exclamation could wonder whether someone is getting injured because of participation in the game or just being threatened with injury. A writer who intended an ongoing transaction rather than a potential one would want to make that clear: "You will avoid willfully inflicting injury upon whomever else is in the game!" Notice that another location signal joins with a different form of an identity signal to work the solution here.

2. Finding Solutions through Dialog with a Reader

Not to put words into your mouth, but imagine a classmate has asked you to help her understand transaction signals better. As you read, you see a mixed signal of transaction and, to help lead your classmate to a better understanding, you pose a question: "What does one side get from the other?"

Writer: I'm not sure what you mean. If there is a transaction going on here, I'm afraid I don't see it: "In rugby, a player who plays on in spite of minor injuries earns bragging rights for he or she."

Reader: Think of the "player" as the actor who receives something later in the sentence. If you were to change the form of "he or she" to create "himself or herself," it combines with "for" and draws attention to how the player becomes the receiver of bragging rights in the transaction.

Writer: Yes, that makes it clearer. I don't see any other mixed signals of transaction.

Reader: Not that many people really spot these in their own writing, and to tell you the truth, some readers miss them also. I do see one right here, in your thesis at the end of your first paragraph: "This makes blogging especially aggressive when the topic is politics, and political blogging seems like a kind of team sport with rough play much like rugby's because upon return for subscribing to the blog, readers get to join the mayhem." I don't see a transaction here either. The question is whether you intend one or not. Are the blog readers just returning from somewhere else, or are they getting something in exchange for subscribing to the blog?

Writer: Oh, they get to join in the verbal bashing if they subscribe to the blog. How would I signal that?

Reader: Think of an alternative to "upon return."

Writer: How about "upon subscribing" or "in exchange for"? What about "in return for"?

Reader: Actually any of those would work. Try one out.

Writer: "This makes blogging especially aggressive when the topic is politics, and political blogging seems like a kind of team sport with rough play much like rugby's because <u>in return</u> for subscribing to the blog, readers get to join the mayhem."

Reader: Yes, the transaction is clearly signaled now. I see two more sentences in this paragraph that need to more clearly signal transaction. Can you spot them?

Writer: I'm not sure.

Reader: Remember this first one, "In rugby, a player who plays on in spite of minor injuries earns bragging rights for <u>him or her</u>"? See if you can apply it to this one: "A player gets the ball down the field past the opposing player at all costs, but the game requires that a player has a lot of knowledge before trying out for a team and avoids willfully inflicting injury toward whoever else is in the game."

Writer: "A player gets the ball down the field past the opposing player at all costs, but the game requires that a player has a lot of knowledge before trying out for a team and avoids willfully inflicting injury <u>upon whomever</u> else is in the game."

Reader: Yes, you spotted "whomever" as opposed to "whoever," just like "him or her" instead of "he or she." You also caught onto using "upon" to replace "toward" like you replaced "toward" with "upon." There are two other words in the sentence that just need to be in a different form.

Writer: Which ones are they?

Reader: "Has" and "avoids" need to change when an action is expected, so "the game requires that a player <u>have</u> a lot of knowledge before trying out for a team and avo<u>id</u> willfully inflicting injury." The last sentence in the paragraph needs the same solution. Give it a try.

Writer: Is it "If every political blogger was to follow that rule, the web would be a better place"?

Reader: Yes, that's it. Give it the same treatment by changing the quantity of the action word like I just did.

Writer: Okay, "If every political blogger <u>were</u> to follow that rule, the web would be a better place."

Reader: Good! You're starting to get it.

Writer: I have one more paragraph to write before this is finished. Can we revisit this writing in a couple of days?

Reader: Sure, no problem, and use what we've just gone over to help with any sentences that need location signals.

Writer: I'll do that, and thanks for the tip.

3. Microlearning Tips for Using what a Reader Has Seen

- When you need to get a reader's feedback on how well you signaled transaction in your own sentences, use this as the next step in developing a sharper eye for seeing mixed signals in your sentences.
- During and after you and a reader sit down together, compare your mixed signals of transaction with your other sentences, especially those which signal transaction clearly.
- Look for who gets it and <u>from whom</u> it comes. Look over your transaction signals when they contain location signals, and mark where in your writing they needed changing and where they did not need changing.
- For instance, see if a sentence of yours expresses some sort of transaction involving something one person gets from another or what one thing gets from another.
- Also be on the lookout for where word forms needed to change because an expectation of action was being expressed.
- The same goes for word forms used for the "receiver" in a transaction.

- If you have begun to see some differences between where you mixed a signal of transaction and where you didn't, use a pen or a highlighter on that piece of writing to write some reminders to look at later.

4. Test Yourself

In thinking about the ways a writer can chose words that clearly signal how one side gets some action or thing from another, look over the "mini-essay" below. If you were a reader in conference with the writer, what options would you suggest that the reader take in swapping the underlined words for clearer signals of transaction? Write your suggestions in the margins below or on a sheet of paper.

Trading Information <u>with</u> Injury

In rugby, a player who plays on in spite of minor injuries earns bragging rights for <u>himself or herself</u>. A political blogger, on the other hand, often begins with bragging and proceeds to inflict injuries upon people who are not there to defend themselves. A blog is shorthand for an online "web log" and it is typically where a "blogger" posts his or her thoughts and where readers respond. This makes blogging especially aggressive when the topic is politics, and political blogging seems like a kind of team sport with rough play much like rugby's because <u>upon return</u> for subscribing to the blog, readers get to join the mayhem.

To compare rugby to blogging one last time, rugby is a physically tough game, mainly because its manner of play is very direct. A player gets the ball down the field past the opposing player at all costs, but the game requires that a player <u>has</u> a lot of knowledge before trying out for a team and <u>avoids</u> willfully inflicting injury <u>toward</u> <u>whomever</u> else is in the game. If every political blogger <u>was</u> to follow that rule, the web would be a better place. The content of many political blogs is downright nasty, with cheap shots being the norm more than the exception.

It's fair to say that written arguments have been around a while. After all, this country was founded and then developed through a series of arguments, some directed <u>at</u> <u>whoever</u> could read them. But rational arguments are not what we always see posted on political blog websites. They seem to bring out the worst in some readers, as if typing nasty comments about politicians they don't like and other readers with <u>who</u> they disagree passes for critical reasoning. Though some blogs are well reasoned, many others read as if the author prefers that a reader <u>remains</u>

as uninformed about history, current events, and economics as possible, as if he or she <u>was</u> a newborn baby that had somehow been born literate. When it comes to responding to what they have read on a blog site, many political bloggers' readers seem to demand that ignorance of the facts <u>is</u> seen as a red badge of courage. Apparently a person doesn't always need to know very much to have an opinion these days.

Once you have written your suggestions for solutions, see "Trading Information for Injury" in appendix three in the appendices in the back of the book.

Sequence

When Things Go out of Order

This is the one signal that is easiest for a reader to spot because it stops the reader cold. It distorts meaning to the point of making a sentence read like some kind of code that has to be deciphered before a reader can continue. Oftentimes, it's simply a matter of the right word in the wrong form ("simple" as opposed to "simply," for instance). Other times, the signal is mixed up because the order of words is mixed up, or a word or several words are missing. This can be the easiest mixed signal to catch when you read your sentences aloud.

There are four ways a sentence usually goes out of sequence, each of them having to do with either the placement of words or their form. These different ways things go out of order in a sentence could be categorized in four ways. The first is the way some sequence mix-ups happen with the writer putting the right word in the wrong place, as with "The toddlers were behaved badly" (the solution being "The toddlers were badly behaved"). In comparison, missing words in a sentence happen at other times, as in "the more know, the faster you learn"). Another way a sentence goes out of sequence is with the right word in the wrong form, for example, "We told her to get here quick," when it should be "We told her to get here quickly." "Sound-alike" words are a fourth way a sentence goes out of sequence: "Their should be a law against this sort of thing" (with "There should be a law against this sort of thing" as the solution).

Each of these four ways a sentence can go out of sequence can arrest a reader's attention because each distorts meaning so much. This chapter will examine all of the ways, offer solutions, and foster improvement in signaling sequence in doing so. Take a few minutes to preview this chapter's four sections, which you will see **numbered and titled in bold**.

1. What Happens when a Signal of Sequence Gets Mixed in a Sentence

Mixed signals of sequence happen in any kind of sentence whether it is a basic sentence or a more developed idea that reads as an expanded version of a basic sentence. When a writer didn't clearly signal sequence in a basic sentence, the mixed signal is often easy to for the reader to see.

Samples of Basic Sentences and Solutions

This first basic sentence sample has all the right words but may give the wrong idea:

I am interesting in photography.

A reader would be justified in wondering whether the writer of this statement is someone who looks <u>interesting</u> or is someone who has an <u>interest</u> in photography. Notice that three different forms of the root word "interest" appear here, two of them with different meanings: "I am interesting in photography" as opposed to "I have an <u>interest</u> in photography," and "I am <u>interested</u> in photography."

This next sample also goes out of sequence because of a single word, but this time, it is not because it's the wrong form of the right word but a wrong word that looks a lot like the right word:

Critical thinking was applied to analyzing the parts of the argument that didn't do nothing.

While Spanish, Italian, and a few other languages allow negative expressions with more than one negative word, only some regional and cultural dialects of English use these "double negatives" while formal written English does not. The writer will need to change one of the negative expressions, either "didn't" or "nothing": "Critical thinking was applied to analyzing the parts of the argument that didn't do <u>anything</u>," or "Critical thinking was applied to analyzing the parts of the argument that <u>did</u> nothing."

This third sample also comes from speaking, this time as a result of the writer using a "sound-alike" word:

She could of written a letter to her employer.

The word "of" is out of sequence with the rest of the sentence because no one "can of written" any more than someone could "of" written. The writer's solution requires exchanging "of" for the word it sounds like, which is "have": "She could <u>have</u> written a letter to her employer."

This next mix-up in signaling sequence happens when a writer identifies something or someone more than necessary:

The more I tried to stay focused, the sleepier I got, so my professor, he saw that and called on me.

Just as Spanish, Italian, and other languages can use double negatives, many languages need a writer to signal identity early in the sentence twice, but English does neither. A reader might wonder if the "he" refers to the professor or not, so by making that clear, the writer would signal sequence clearly: "The more I tried to stay focused, the sleepier I got, so my <u>professor saw</u> that and called on me."

This last basic sentence sample is missing a word, thereby throwing the sentence out of sequence:

By playing Ping-Pong, I learned how to think quickly, strategize, and hand-eye coordination.

The first two of the three things the writer learned are actions, "think quickly" and "strategize," so the third must be an action as well, something like "<u>use</u> hand-eye coordination."

Samples of Expanded Sentences and Solutions

Developing what would otherwise be a basic sentence into an expanded sentence means a writer has more to check when it comes to signaling sequence. This first <u>way</u> one runs into trouble <u>is the same</u> way that one of the previous basic sentence samples did:

The exam it was hard, so hard that I didn't see any clues in some of the questions that I could use to figure out answers to other questions, which made me confusing.

Like the earlier sample that used "my professor, he saw," adding an extra identity signal into the sentence, with both "exam" and "it" mixes the sequence signal. If a reader advised the writer to delete one of them, the logical choice would be "it" since "exam" is the "actor" in the sentence and is identified there: "<u>The exam was hard</u>, so hard that I didn't see any clues in some of the questions that I could use to figure out answers to other questions, which made me confusing." The writer should consider the form of his or her sentence's last word as well—unless the writer actually became a confusing person and not a person who was <u>confused</u>.

This next sample of an expanded sentence is missing a word, if not several words:

I'm convinced that video game, I got a basic understanding of traffic management, micro-economics, and urban planning, so I'm going to put it on my resumé and see what happens.

The sentence's sequence breaks down right at the start. Since experience with a single video game is the way the sentence's author learned so much, he or she may need to add either a location signal ("<u>from</u> that video game") or an action ("by playing" or "as a result of playing") and possibly a quantity signal with it (for "<u>the</u> video game). There are three possible solutions, then:

I'm convinced that <u>from</u> that video game, I got a basic understanding of traffic management, micro-economics, and urban planning, so I'm going to put it on my resumé and see what happens;

I'm convinced that <u>by playing the</u> video game, I got a basic understanding of traffic management, micro-economics, and urban planning, so I'm going to put it on my resumé and see what happens;

I'm convinced that <u>as a result of playing the</u> video game, I got a basic understanding of traffic management, micro-economics, and urban planning, so I'm going to put it on my resumé and see what happens;

Next comes an expanded sentence sample with the right word in the wrong form:

The odd license plate numbers were usable every other day starting from Monday and the even plate numbers were usable on the remainder days of the week.

This mixed signal doesn't distort meaning as much as missing words affect sequence, but it will distract a reader away from what the writer wants to communicate. The solution means telling the writer that "remainder" just needs a different form: "The odd license plate numbers were usable every other day starting from Monday and the even plate numbers were usable on the <u>remaining</u> days of the week." Bear in mind that "remainder" and "remaining" both describe the days the writer obviously means, but only "remaining" will fit into that place before "days" to keep the sentence in sequence.

This last expanded sentence sample contains a mixed signal of sequence that can slip by a reader who reads too quickly:

What concerned me right away was that the staff at Happy Hare Day Care had fewer staff members with Early Childhood Education credentials then the other day care center I evaluated as one of my assignments for this class.

Instead of "than," the person who wrote the sentence put "then," a time signal where no time signal could be in a sentence. That could be explained by how much "then" and "than" sound alike.

Samples of Questions, Directions, and Exclamations

Each of the previous sample sentences is a statement, the most common kind of sentence. Questions, directives (sometimes called "commands"), and exclamations of shock or surprise can also have mixed signals of sequence. These first four samples are questions.

Questions

This first two are rephrased versions of the first two basic sentence samples. Compare these with their statement versions, and take notice that the difference between a statement and a question can depend on sequence. Like its statement version, this first question creates a mystery about what the writer really wants to know:

Are you interesting in photography?

As mentioned earlier, the person reading this question could very well wonder just what the questioner is asking. The form of the word "interest" is a problem in that two forms of it, "interesting" and "interested" have completely different meanings. If the questioner actually meant to ask whether or not the reader wanted to take photographs or learn about photography, he or she would have to change the word's form so that the signal was in sequence with the question's intended meaning: "Are you interested in photography?"

This next question's sample borrows from the "double negative" that inhabited the statement version:

Isn't critical thinking developed by analyzing the parts of the argument that didn't do nothing else?

Formal written English does not allow double negatives even though they may be perfectly acceptable to speakers and listeners in some local areas. For that reason, a reader might ask the writer about the intended audience for the question. If the question was meant not just for people who use double negatives in their everyday conversation but also people from everywhere else, the best advice would be to go with formality: "Isn't critical thinking developed by analyzing the parts of the argument that didn't do <u>anything</u> else?"

Unlike "then," "than," and some other "sound-alike words that can be difficult to catch at first glance, this mixed signal of sequence practically leaps off the page:

Don't you think you learned more your mistakes to strengthen your weaknesses?

This reads like the basic sentence was the core of the writer's idea: "Don't you think you learned more?" As he or she expanded the basic sentence, sequence became mixed as details like "strengthen" mixed with "weaknesses." The reader may want to advise the writer to add missing location signals, "from" and "in" to a new form of "strengthen": "Don't you think you learned more <u>from</u> your mistakes <u>in</u> strengthen<u>ing</u> your weaknesses?"

This last question reads as breakdown in word sequence as well:

So if the brain is to busy in the addiction, how could critical thinking skills be developed?

On closer inspection, a reader may see that the sequence mix-up comes from "to" sitting where "too" should be: "the brain is <u>too</u> busy."

Directions

As usual, a statement with directive intent is meant for the reader and expects some kind of action. They can be phrased so they take on the tone of a command or, like this first sample, offer advice:

Travel on the "three ships" in college, assistantship, scholarship, and working as an intern.

The advice is clear enough, but words in a list should be in the same form as much as possible. After checking a dictionary, the writer would find that he or she can list all three of the "ships" with the same last syllable: "Travel on the "three ships" in college, assistantship, scholarship, and intern*ship*."

This next one also has a mixed signal of sequence, but not because of a word's form:

For this assignment chose a sports team here at Big State College, a team it is representative.

The sentence goes out of sequence when "it" appears after "team." One test a reader could suggest is removing the word that mixes sequence and replacing it with a blank: "For this assignment chose a sports team here at Big State College, a team _____ is representative." Then the directive's writer might try some words that typically link a thing like "team" with the words that describe it, "a team <u>that</u> is representative," "a team <u>that</u> is <u>considered</u> representative," "a team <u>being</u> representative," or even "a team <u>is</u> representative," to list but four possibilities. Getting some more feedback from the reader would probably lead to the right linking word: "For this assignment chose a sports team here at Big State College, a team <u>that</u> is representative."

Like the first sample of a directive sentence, this one has the right word in the wrong form:

Let the audience know what you are trying to reveal, whether it is enthusiastic, bravery, or sorrow.

The three personal qualities are clear, but the directive doesn't read well with "enthusiastic" in a different form than "bravery" and "sorrow." Again a quick field trip to the dictionary would be good advice to give to the writer. One of two solutions could come of it: "Let the audience know what you are trying to reveal, whether it is enthusia<u>sm</u>, bravery, or sorrow," or "Let the audience know what you are trying to reveal, whether it is <u>feeling</u> enthusiastic, <u>brave</u>, or <u>sorry</u>." Notice that the second solution needed a "helping" word.

This last one reads as a case of the right word in the wrong form, but the culprit is a "sound-alike" word that the writer chose but probably did not mean:

Remember, you are apart of a large organization.

A reader could wonder whether the sentence is out of sequence because of location (which could be "apart <u>from</u> a large organization") or because of a "sound-alike" word (as in "<u>a part</u> of a large organization"). A reader will need to ask about the sequence of words since a person is either being directed to feel like he or she is <u>a part of</u> an organization or <u>apart from</u> it in response to this directive.

Exclamations

Like directions, exclamations of shock or surprise are written to prompt a response from the reader, in some cases, an emotional response. The first one follows the habits of casual speech:

Good thing I checked out this day care center!

People often shorten exclamations, omitting words to get the sentence across quickly and increase the dramatic effect. A reader should remind the writer of this common habit, and encourage using the missing words in a way that doesn't sacrifice the sense of urgency. One solution might look like this: "<u>It's</u> a good thing I checked out this day care center!"

This one is even more of a puzzle than the last question sample:

This is apart from the barbecue!

With "from" and "apart," any reader should ask whether the writer meant something separate from the barbecue or one of the parts that goes to the barbecue. Like the solution to "you are apart of a large organization," knowing the reader's intended meaning will send the sequence one way or the other: "This is <u>a part</u> from the barbecue!"or "This is <u>apart</u> from the barbecue!"

2. Finding Solutions through Dialog with a Reader

This middle part of this chapter demonstrates the value of a reader who provides reactions and suggestions a reader can use to spot and repair mixed signals of sequence. Not having a university degree in English shouldn't disqualify someone from serving as the reader because any person with a high level of English speaking, reading, and writing skills who honestly wants to help can be an excellent reader of a student's sentences. For example, imagine that a friend has asked you to help spot mixed signals of sequence in an assignment for an Early Child-hood Education class. After taking a minute or two to look over the assignment, you see a sentence that prompts you to ask,

"What order of thoughts do you mean?"

Writer: I'm not sure I see anything not in order. What do you see?

Reader: It's this sentence in your first paragraph. I'll use a different tone of voice and really emphasize the pronunciation when I get to the spot where it goes out of sequence, so you'll hear it: "What concerned me right away was that the staff at Happy Hare Day Care had fewer staff members with Early Childhood Education credentials *then* the other day care center I evaluated as one of my assignments for this class."

Writer: Oh, I meant "than."

Reader: Right, you caught it. "Then" and "than" sound very muck alike. There's another one of these two paragraphs later, but the wrong word and the right word sound so much alike that I'll just have to point to it here on the page. Do you mean "apart" as in "separate" or "a part" as in a component?

Writer: It does really stare right back at me now that I look at it. It should say "Staff supervision is a part of the problem," not "Staff supervision is *apart* of the problem."

Reader: Yes, that's good. Here is one more sound-alike in your last paragraph, and I bet you'll see it right away: "I'm not arguing that day care professionals should be up on a pedal stool, but they should at least be credentialed and be supervised by a licensed operator."

Writer: Wow! I can't believe I wrote that! Yes, it should be "I'm not arguing that day care professionals should be up on a pedestal, but they should at least be credentialed and be supervised by a licensed operator."

Yes, now the sequence signal in the sentence works well. Here's a different kind of mixed sequence signal: "The staff, they seemed more interested in chatting with one another than monitoring the children's activities."

Writer: Why is it out of sequence?

Reader: You name what we could call this sentence's "main actor" twice: "The staff, they." Which identity is the more necessary of the two?

Writer: I guess I could just use "they" since the sentence before and after make it pretty clear that I mean the facility's staff. So "They seemed more interested in chatting with one another than monitoring the children's activities" would be the solution?

Reader: Yes, that would fix it. Here's a mixed signal of sequence happening because the right word is in the wrong form. I'll read it and emphasize the word when I get to it: "The staff should be more *focus* on engaging the children in activities."

Writer: That should be focused. Are there any more?

Reader: I just see one more, a case of missing words only because you are writing for a class assignment instead of just saying it in conversation: "Good thing I checked out this day care center!"

Writer: Words are missing? How about "<u>It's a</u> good thing I checked out this day care center!"

Reader: That's perfect, good job. You seem to have gotten better at straightening out the sequence signals.

Writer: Yes, I think so. Maybe next time we'll try to see if I can spot more mixed signals of sequence.

Reader: That sounds like a plan. Just let me know when you're ready.

Writer: Yes, I will.

3. Microlearning Tips for Using what a Reader Has Seen

- When you need to get a reader's feedback on how well you signal sequence in your own sentences, use it as the next step in developing a sharper eye for seeing mixed signals in your sentences.
- During and after you and a reader sit down together, compare the ways you mixed signals of sequence—word forms, word order, missing words, or "sound-alike" words. Write which particular way in the margins of the page next to the sentence where it occurred. Look for any sentences where sequence of thoughts and words clearly signaled what you meant, and look for differences.
- If you had mixed signals of sequence because you used the right word but put it in the wrong form, make a note that shows the original sentence, the solution, and as many forms of the word as you can find in a dictionary.
- If word order was an issue, write down the original sentence, the solution, and as many ways of saying the same thing in different words that come to mind.

- Do the same for any sentences that were out of sequence because they were missing one or more words.
- Make a list of any "sound-alike" words that your reader spotted in your writing.

4. Test Yourself

See if you can think of the changes needed to clear up the mixed signals of sequence underlined in this short essay. Write your solutions in the margins below or on a sheet of paper.

Putting Things in Order

When I started college, I wanted to look a little more into it <u>then</u> other students because I believed that it wasn't only <u>myself</u> helping <u>me</u> succeed. I was a <u>student</u> serious, but that school seemed nothing like I had imagined it would be. No one could <u>of</u> imagined what a <u>strain</u> experience it would be for me.

During the first week of classes, the parking enforcement staff diligently responded to students' attempts at creative parking, towing <u>there</u> cars one by one. Fortunately, I didn't have to worry about parking at Big State University because I was able to take public transportation and get there <u>quick</u>. <u>Alot</u> of the students were walking around like zombies. <u>All most</u> none of them could find the classes they needed and just <u>seamed</u> disoriented and <u>desparated</u> as they hiked from one side of the campus to the other in pursuit of classes with empty seats.

Not that a seat in a classroom was anything special since the walls of one of my classrooms had pictures of the outside <u>were</u> there should <u>of</u> been windows. It turned out that I wasn't the only serious student in my classes. It turned out that a lot of the chatter in the back of the classroom was among students who were answering questions and <u>shared</u> notes from the last class meeting. I was right about success not coming without the help of others.

You can peek at "Putting Things in Order" in appendix three if you just want to see the solutions to this self-test, but this might not be the best time to take shortcuts. Learning to improve sentences takes time, patience, and honesty.

Relation

Relating the Parts

Writers need to clearly signal how sentence parts relate to one another.

The two main ways this signal gets mixed up. An incomplete sentence is one way (an example of which appears just before this sentence). The other way is when a sentence has more than one group of words that could be a sentence by itself, then the relation of sentence parts needs clarifying (with this sentence standing as a prime example). When the solution to a mixed signal of relation appears as an incomplete sentence, the solution typically involves joining it to a neighboring sentence, while the solution to two or more sentences appearing as one sentence involves either creating separate sentences or connecting groups of words within that sentence, which can be as simple as adding a connecting word like "and," "because," or "but," to name just three from a very long list of possibilities, or beginning a sentence like this one with a certain kind of connecting word. Notice that the previous sentence, as long as it is, has clear signals of relation wherever they are needed. Connecting words ("while" and "which") made that possible.

The source of the problem may be the difference between spoken and written sentences. Consider how spoken sentences obviously do not need punctuation or capital letters, so "That is my seat yours is over there" communicates the message accurately when spoken, especially with a pause at just the right time, yet it needs a signal of relation when expressed on the page: "That is my seat, and yours is over there." The same goes for statements like "People who are looking right at you aren't necessarily paying attention to what you are saying something to remember when giving directions." On the page, it would need a signal of relation: "People who are looking right at you aren't necessarily paying attention to what you are saying, something to remember when giving directions." Notice that a comma solved the problem while a period in the wrong place would not: "People who are looking right at you aren't necessarily paying attention to what you are saying. Something to remember when giving directions."

This chapter will show what you need to remember when you need to signal the relation between sentence parts. Take a few minutes to preview this chapter's four sections, which you will see **numbered and titled in bold**.

1. What Happens when a Signal of Relation Gets Mixed in a Sentence

Even though there are just two ways a writer's intended meaning does not get clearly signaled, mixed signals of relation can be tricky to catch. This is because more than any of the other six ways writers signal meaning, relation seems clear enough when spoken.

Samples of Basic Sentences and Solutions

This first basic sentence sample shows what happens when a writer stops a sentence a little too soon:

The increasing appeal of reality-type television shows to many audiences.

Either this sentence stopped too soon, or one before it did. For instance, one solution a reader could advise the writer to consider would be practical if the previous sentence said, "The increase in the number of unemployed actors could be explained." Then they could be combined: "The increase in the number of unemployed actors <u>could be explained by</u> the increasing appeal of reality-type television shows to many audiences."

Unlike the previous sample, this one's relation breaks down not because a sentence stopped too soon, but because it needed to stop sooner or just needs a relation signal:

Compliments are like pimples, everyone gets them in different places.

A reader and the sentence's writer could talk about which of six possible solutions would best fit the paragraph the sentence inhabits. Five of them use a connecting word: "Compliments are like pimples as everyone gets them in different places"; "Compliments are like pimples, for everyone gets them in different places"; "Compliments are like pimples since everyone gets them in different places"; "Compliments are like pimples, so everyone gets them in different places"; (and) "Compliments are like pimples because everyone gets them in different places."

Bear in mind that "as," "for," "since," and "so" have similar meanings and signal that the relation between sentence parts is a matter of cause-and-effect. On the other hand, though "because" also signals the cause-and-effect relation between sentence parts, it emphasizes the importance of the part that follows it, implying that the reader may not already know about the getting compliments (or pimples) in different places.

One more potential solution to the mixed signal of relation here relies on a semicolon rather than a connecting word:

"Compliments are like pimples; everyone gets them in different places." Unlike the other possible solutions, the semicolon neither shows a cause-and effect relation between the two sentence parts nor implies that one part is more important than the other. It simply solves the problem of keeping the two parts separate while still keeping them in the same sentence. The writer might choose a semicolon if he or she did not want to suggest a case-and-effect relation. This option and a similar one using a colon can be found in appendix one, "Punctuation and the Seven Signals."

This next basic sentence sample suffers from a similar problem:

All eight of my friends decided to try skydiving, now there are seven.

As with the previous sample, the writer could just choose to create two separate sentences or use a semicolon, but he or she might want to signal cause-and-effect with "as," "since," "so," or even "because." Alternately, "and" would signal the relation between sentence parts, also meaning cause-and-effect, but would highlight the result as well: "All eight of my friends decided to try skydiving, <u>and</u> now there are seven" (to emphasize the result of having one less friend).

This last basic sentence sample shows a mixed signal of relation that can escape a writer's eye:

Something that everyone needs to watch for and is a problem for everyone, young and old.

By itself, it has the feel of a slogan, yet it seems to flow from the sentence before it, which makes the relation seem already clear. As a separate, free-standing sentence, though, it is not complete. The writer has two options for signaling relation, one being connecting it to the previous sentence: "This last basic sentence sample shows a mixed signal of sequence that can escape a writer's <u>eye, something</u> that everyone needs to watch for and is a problem for everyone, young and old." The other solution would be to add enough words so it could stand alone: "<u>This is</u> something that everyone needs to watch for and is a problem for everyone, young and old."

Samples of Expanded Sentences and Solutions

Expanding what would have been a basic sentence by adding more details means a writer needs to more carefully check for any missing signals of the relation of sentence parts. This first expanded sentence resembles the two of the basic samples since it contains elements of more than one complete sentence:

I buy just one lottery ticket every payday a dollar for hope has more value than a hundred dollars for desperation.

The person who wrote this sentence coupled two complete but related thoughts together into one sentence. Once a reading of the sentence reveals that particular kind of mixed relation of sentence parts, the writer will need to consider which solution best fits the way he or she wants the sentence to read. As mentioned before, the writer could also take what might seem like the easy way out by just adding a semicolon between the two parts that read as complete sentences: "I buy just one lottery ticket every payday; a dollar for hope has more value than a hundred dollars for desperation." As also mentioned before, the writer could use a connecting word that accurately expresses the meaning behind how the sentence parts relate to each other. For instance, "because" not only shows a cause-and-effect relation but emphasizes the importance of the second part to a reader who may have known about it: "I buy just one lottery ticket every payday because a dollar for hope has more value than a hundred dollars for desperation. Alternate solutions could involve "as," "for," "since," or "and."

Keep in mind that not every possible connecting word is equal. Some are a good fit in a sentence needing a relation signal while others are not. Take the example of the connecting word "but," a solution that would put the two sentence parts in conflict with each other: "I buy just one lottery ticket every payday, but a dollar for hope has more value than a hundred dollars for desperation." One better solution would use one of the choices from the previous paragraph: "I buy just one lottery ticket every payday since a dollar for hope has more value than a hundred dollars for desperation."

This next sample has the same kind of problem, but the comma draws a reader's attention to the point where the relation signal is missing:

Nothing livens up a pool party like a drunk on a diving board, nothing puts a damper on a party like yellow police tape.

The repeated word "nothing" makes the sentence read like a list, and that might explain why mixed signals of relation like this get past a writer's eye. The comma points the way to the mix-up though since the words before and after it could each stand as a separate sentence. Like the solution, "All eight of my friends decided to try skydiving, <u>and</u> now there are seven," using "and" could draw attention to the logical outcome: "Nothing livens up a pool party like a drunk on a diving board, <u>and</u> nothing puts a damper on a party like yellow police tape."

This expanded sentence sample is borrowed from this chapter's first paragraph:

The other way is when a sentence has more than one group of words that could be a sentence by itself, then the relation of sentence parts needs clarifying.

A reader might have an easy time spotting the problem here if the sentence were back in the paragraph where it originally appeared, which was a paragraph discussing and demonstrating mixed signals of relation. Like the previous sentence sample, the comma could tip off a reader that the relation between two parts of the sentence needs signaling. Since "then" highlights the outcome, a semicolon could be the writer's first choice for a solution: "The other way is when a sentence has more than one group of words that could be a sentence by <u>itself; then</u> the relation of sentence parts needs clarifying."

This last one might seem like a complete sentence because it is so long:

While earth scientists predicted Mt. Aetna's ongoing eruption when there were tremors within the mountain and bulges in the ground long before things started happening.

The sample's length helps explain why a careful reader may spot the mixed relation signal, an incomplete sentence, more readily than its author could have. With a mix-up like this, the solution will always come with the same two options, namely connecting it to a neighboring sentence, or either adding or removing enough words so it could stand alone: "While earth scientists predicted how Mt. Aetna's ongoing eruption when there were tremors within the mountain and bulges in the ground long before things started happening, <u>they neglected to inform local authorities who would need to get residents evacuated</u>," or

"<u>Earth</u> scientists predicted Mt. Aetna's ongoing eruption when there were tremors within the mountain and bulges in the ground long before things started happening."

Samples of Questions, Directions, and Exclamations

While the basic and extended sample sentences in this chapter are statements, mixed signals of relation do come along in other kinds of sentences, namely questions, directions, and exclamations of shock or surprise. These first four samples are questions.

Questions

The question, "What *relation* of sentence parts does the writer seem to mean?" would be worth asking here:

How are compliments like pimples, everyone gets them in different places?

Like the earlier version of this question that appeared as a basic sentence sample, the relation of sentence parts is unclear because the sentence needs to stop sooner or just needs a connecting word. The solution of stopping sooner would mean the writer could opt for two questions: "How are compliments like <u>pimples? Is</u> it that everyone gets them in different places?" Alternately, both sentence parts would need a connecting word like "since": "How are compliments like pimples <u>since</u> everyone gets them in different places?" Notice that the comma had to go. Also, a connecting word like "that" will work as a solution: "How are compliments like pimples <u>that</u> everyone gets in different places?" For this solution to work, "them" as well as the comma between "pimples" and "everyone" would have to go.

This second question also appeared earlier in this chapter:

So something that everyone needs to watch for and is a problem for everyone, young and old?

Unlike the statement version of this question here, the word "so" could act as a solution after the writer has removed the later connecting word, "and": "So something that everyone needs to watch <u>for is</u> a problem for everyone, young and old?" Notice that "and" didn't signal the relation between sentence parts because the sample is not a complete sentence, so removing it creates a basic sentence: "Something that everyone needs to watch for is a problem for everyone, young and old." The question version here needs "so" at the beginning to make a question and does not really serve here as a connecting word.

The next question presents a similar problem to the first question in this section, namely whether the question can stand separately or not:

If the volcanologist voiced the likelihood of an eruption to her colleagues and publically presented her findings in a very clever way, did alarm the public?

Since the question here cannot stand alone, it needs attaching to a neighboring sentence or enough added words that can make it stand alone. Since the question is fairly long already, the writer may decide to first ask it and then come up with an answer, so he or she would need to add an "actor" to the second part: " If the volcanologist voiced the likelihood of an eruption to her colleagues, and publically presented her findings in a very clever way, did <u>she</u> alarm the public?"

This last question may look familiar:

What *relation* of sentence parts?

Of course the solution could just be to join this to a neighboring sentence: "<u>When seeing a question about signaling the relation of sentence parts, a reader might ask a question</u>, what *relation* of sentence parts?" But the writer could intend to ask the question first and then provide an answer. In that case, the solution could be, "<u>When seeing a question about signaling the relation of sentence parts, a reader might wonder</u>, 'what *relation* of sentence parts?'"

Directions

These next two samples appear among the four questions above, taken and re-phrased as commands or directives below.

Though no longer a question, this one looks quite different from its earlier statement version:

State on your application how compliments are like pimples, everyone can get them in different places.

The possible solutions listed with the statement version earlier in this chapter included a list of connecting words between the two parts of the sentence that could stand as sentences by themselves, and the same solution could work here: "State on your application how are compliments like pimples, <u>and</u> everyone can get them in different places." There are other options for connecting words here, like "because," "since," "as" and "for."

One test a writer can use to see whether to use a connecting word is to look for how many parts of a sentence could actually stand alone. Think of how even the most basic sentence must have two components, the "actor," the person or thing doing something in the sentence, and the "action," what the actor is doing. For example, since this directive sentence assumes that the reader must do something, the actor is "you," the reader: " (You) state on your application how compliments are like pimples," the action being to state how. The other part contains an actor, "everyone" and an action, "can get": "everyone can get them in different places."

That test also works when a sentence is incomplete, like this directive:

Something that you need to watch for and is a problem for everyone, young and old.

There is an actor, the "something" that you the reader need to watch for, and while there is an "action," "watch," there is no central action unless words get added: "<u>There is</u> something that you need to watch for and is a problem for everyone, young and old." "Is" tells a reader what "something" is doing, namely being the focus of the sentence.

Exclamations

These last two samples are phrased as exclamations that express shock or surprise. This first one will stop a reader right away:

The two main ways this signal gets mixed up!

That reader would probably look for a nearby sentence to see where the central "actor" and "act" are. If the writer prefers a separate sentence though, the reader could suggest adding words and trying a different beginning. In response, the reader might try "<u>There are</u> two main ways this signal gets mixed up!"

The next expression of shock or surprise would trigger a reader's response if he or she were to run the actor/action test:

This is alarming the volcanologist voiced the likelihood of an eruption to her colleagues!

Since "This is alarming" has an actor ("this") and an action ("is"), this part of the sentence could also stand alone, so the directive needs a connecting word: "This is alarming <u>because</u> the volcanologist voiced the likelihood of an eruption to her colleagues!"

2. Finding Solutions through Dialog with a Reader

This part of the chapter demonstrates how a writer can enlist a reader's help in locating mixed signals of relation. Someone doesn't need to have a degree in English to play the role of the reader. Any person with a high level of English speaking, reading, and writing skills who honestly wants to help can serve as a reader of a student's sentences. The reader's task here is to look for a mixed signal of meaning, the relation between sentence parts in this case, and bring it to the writer's attention when one appears. Starting with a question helps a writer to focus on the sentence and recall what he or she meant. Upon seeing a mixed signal of relation in a sentence, a reader might very well ask, "What *relation* of sentence parts do you mean?"

Writer: I'm not sure which parts you are asking about.

Reader: Let's take a look at this sentence in your first paragraph: "While earth scientists predicted Mt. Aetna's ongoing eruption when there were tremors within the mountain and bulges in the ground long before things started happening." Look at the parts, "While earth scientists predicted Mt. Aetna's ongoing eruption," and "when there were tremors within the mountain and bulges in the ground long before things started happening." Could either part stand as a sentence by itself?

Writer: No, and I see that together they wouldn't be a complete sentence either.

Reader: That's right. Could a word be taken out or added to solve the problem?

Writer: Maybe if we take "while" out, move "when," and add a comma, it will work: "When earth scientists predicted Mt. Aetna's ongoing <u>eruption, there</u> were tremors within the mountain and bulges in the ground long before things started happening."

Reader: That seems like the simplest solution. Otherwise, you'd have to add a lot of words to the front end of the sentence.

Yes, I'd probably have to add something like "The signs were there." The first way is better. Do you see any more?

Reader: I see just two more. Here's one in the second paragraph, and it's a lot like the one we just saw: "The volcanologist presenting her findings in a very clever way, not alarming the public but bringing the likelihood of an eruption to her colleagues.

Writer: I think just a slight change would fix it, something like this: "The volcanologist <u>presented</u> her findings in a very clever way, not alarming the public but bringing the likelihood of an eruption to her colleagues."

Reader: Yes, good, now the volcanologist is *doing* something rather than just being a part of someone else's action. There is just one more.

Writer: This must be it: "If the geological community agrees with this statement, and all of the seismic data matches the results of the data are obtained from surface measurements."

Reader: Yes, that's the one. Is there more to the "if" part?

Writer: Yes, it follows that part as a separate sentence. How about "If the geological community agrees with this statement, and all of the seismic data matches the results of the data obtained from surface measurements, <u>vital information will get pooled together to improve the prediction of volcanic eruption</u>."

Reader: Yes, that's perfect. Unless you have any other concerns, we're done.

3. Microlearning Tips for Using what a Reader Has Seen

- When you need to get a reader's response to mixed signals of relation in your own sentences, use that as the next step in developing a sharper eye for seeing them.
- During and after you and a reader sit down together, compare your mixed signals of relation with your other sentences.
- It's pretty unlikely that you mixed up every single relation signal in a piece of writing, especially if you wrote a paragraph or more. Look at how some of your sentences did in fact signal the relation between sentence parts correctly by using connecting words or clearly relating sentence parts.
- Use those instances of correctness to guide you in clearly signaling relation more consistently. For instance, if you forgot a connecting word between two word groups that could be sentences by themselves, make the correction and make a note of the "before" and "after" of the problem sentence and its solution. If you composed

an incomplete sentence, also make a "before" and "after" history of the problem and its solution.

- In solving these sorts of mixed relation problems, there is a test you can run that may help you spot sentences needing more attention. One way to check both for both kinds is to think of a basic sentence as having an "actor" as well as an "action." Take any of the sentence samples in the chapter, and notice how the absence of either an actor or action made a sentence incomplete, or how a connecting word was needed when there were pair of actors and actions within a sentence. Test your own sentences for actors and actions.
- If you have begun to see some differences between where you mixed a signal of relation and where you didn't, use a pen or a highlighter on that piece of writing to write some reminders to look at later.

4. Test Yourself

Imagine for the next few minutes that you wrote the short essay below and you are working with a reader in locating and solving mixed signals of relation. As you see the mixed signals of relation, correct them, and circle the corrections with a pencil, not a pen. Just a few of the many choices of connecting words will work as solutions to those sentences where a connecting word is needed: "and," "so," "because," "but," or "since." Of course, any case of a sentence not being complete will need some consideration of where and how to attach it to a neighboring sentence.

Relating to Beautiful People

Often thought of as "the beautiful people," celebrities appear on television, highway billboards, glossy magazine covers, and other places as well dressed, well groomed, and well, beautiful. More of these people are spotted in our local convenience stores and supermarkets than almost anywhere else on the planet, my fellow Californians and I should divulge a dirty little secret. They don't look all that glamorous pushing their carts through the produce section or making a late-night stop for a half-gallon of milk. Aside from the unnoticeable closed-circuit security camera. Celebrities need to look good in front of cameras, that affects their ability to stay in the public eye. They have to look beautiful for commercial reasons. Not to degrade the value of one of our state's biggest exports, right up there with pesticide-free lettuce, organic tomatoes, and hormone-free chicken breasts. The rest of the world should know that Hollywood types use the services of health spas (a.k.a. "fat farms") and migrant skin care workers who go to exfoliate, trim, or spray as needed. These services are available to the public, for a price of course, most of us will admit to needing a little improving now and then.

You can peek at "Relating to Beautiful People" in appendix three if you just want to see the solutions to this self-test, but try to resist the temptation to use it to short-circuit your learning.

No written sentence is possible without punctuation. Besides using periods to mark the end of a sentence, other pieces of punctuation mark words or phrases within sentences. Many of these punctuation marks play a role in signaling the intended meaning.

Apostrophes

Apostrophes keep sequence and quantity straight. Sometimes a word has an apostrophe at its end even though no ownership is involved, which creates a mixed signal of sequence. See what happens when apostrophes run amok this way:

What American's have yet to discover are all of the possible uses for bubble wrap.

Remember, no shirt, no shoe's, no service.

Since the intended word was "Americans" (as in many of them) and "shoes" (as in a pair of them), the quantity signal is as mixed up as the sequence signal.

When a writer does mean ownership and there is more than one, the apostrophe should follow the "s":

In which fantasy education system would <u>students'</u> test scores be higher?

A missing apostrophe can mix-up sequence as much as an unnecessary one:

The street vendor emphasized, "I dont use no double negatives when I say to someone, 'I dont have no change.'"

Another use for apostrophes is a quotation-within-a-quotation. In a sample borrowed from the chapter on relation, the quoted sentence itself quotes a reader who asks, "What *relation* of sentence parts?" Putting the question within apostrophes inside of the quoted sentence tells readers that the quoted sentence was doing some quoting as well: "When seeing a question about signaling the relation of sentence parts, a reader might ask, 'What *relation* of sentence parts?'

Commas

Commas seem to give writers more trouble than any other kind of punctuation. They get overdone, misplaced, or omitted, usually because a writer doesn't have a way of testing a sentence to see whether or not it needs a comma. Most comma errors happen for just three reasons. Two have to do with signaling sequence, and the other has a link to transaction.

Items in a List

Remember this one? "On the first day of Christmas, my true love gave to me five golden rings, four calling birds, three French hens, two turtle doves and a partridge in a pear tree." The problem here is that a missing comma alters the meaning since the partridge was all by itself in the pear tree. That's the rule, then. In this way, the intended sequence signal is clear: "On the first day of Christmas, my true love gave to me five golden rings, four calling birds, three French hens, two turtle doves, and a partridge in a pear tree."

Just-to-Clarify

Take a close look at this kind of sentence, where some information appears in the midst of everything: "That famous soft drink 'sip test,' in which people taking a sip of one brand of soda pop always liked it better than a sip of another brand, was really product promotion disguised as consumer research." Yes, one could simply say, "That famous soft drink 'sip test' was really product promotion disguised as consumer research," but adding that bit of clarification about how the sip test actually worked would reveal more purpose as to what the writer is saying here. Reading it in the shortened version happens to work as a test of where the commas needed to go, namely around the words that could be removed without affecting the sequence of the rest of the sentence. Reading it without any commas at all and then comparing it to the corrected version demonstrates how the "just-to-clarify" commas keep sequence straight. Words run together without the commas: "That famous soft drink "sip test" in which people taking a sip of one brand of soda pop always liked it better than a sip of <u>another brand was really</u> product promotion disguised as consumer research." The underlined words show where the sequence gets confounded. With the commas in the right places, sequence is clear: "That famous soft drink 'sip test,' in which people taking a sip of one brand of soda pop always liked it better than a sip of another brand, was really product promotion disguised as consumer research."

Situation and Result

This type of comma use signals transaction: "When you check your grammar, be sure your context, organization, and support are all strong first." Okay, look at the sentence and notice that even though the situation part, "when you check your grammar," should chronologically happen last, it is the situation that the rest of that sentence follows.

Here's an easier one, so try to guess where a comma should go between the situation and its result: "Since the semester started the reading has required more logical analysis and more creative reasoning." If you guessed that the comma needs to go between "started" and "the," you sensed how the situation ends, and where the "result" part starts and needs a comma to mark the spot. Without the comma, the intended transaction, the passing of time and the difference in the difficulty of the reading, is all but invisible. Here it is with the comma: "Since the semester started, the reading has required more logical analysis and more creative reasoning."

Parentheses

Take one more look at this sentence from the section on commas: "That famous soft drink 'sip test,' in which people taking a sip of one brand of soda pop always liked it better than a sip of another brand, was really product promotion disguised as consumer research." Besides using "just-to-clarify" commas, a writer can opt for parentheses for the same reason, namely placing added information in the sentence without disrupting sequence: "That famous soft drink 'sip test' (in which people taking a sip of one brand of soda pop always liked it better than a sip of another brand) was really product promotion disguised as consumer research."

Semicolons and Colons

One sentence from the chapter on relation illustrates how these two very useful pieces of punctuation sort out the relation between sentence parts:

"Compliments are like pimples; everyone gets them in different places."

Though it doesn't explain the relation between two parts that could stand separately as sentences, the semicolon separates them enough to make the sentence work. A writer can change a semicolon to a colon if the second part explains the first: "Compliments are like pimples: everyone gets them in different places."

A semicolon can also separate items in a list that have their own commas, as shown in the short demonstration of connecting words in the chapter on relation.

Five of them use a connecting word: "Compliments are like pimples as everyone gets them in different places"; "Compliments are like pimples, for everyone gets them in different places," "Compliments are like pimples since everyone gets them in different places"; "Compliments are like pimples, so everyone gets them in different places," (and)

"Compliments are like pimples, <u>because</u> everyone gets them in different places."

Hyphens

Hyphens help signal sequence when the order of words could distort their intended meaning. For instance, compare two versions of this sentence: "The relation between rugby and mayhem is a matter of cause and effect." "The relation between rugby and mayhem is a matter of cause-and-effect." Without the hyphens, "cause-and-effect" doesn't seem like a whole process as much as two separate items, "cause" and "effect."

A hyphen also joins two or more separate words into one compound word with a single meaning: "Over a period of six months, the company's casual Friday gradually began to look like a come-as-you-are party." This also applies to numbers like thirty-six.

Dashes

A dash puts a sentence on "pause"—a stop that is shorter and not as final as a period but longer than a comma. Consider how this sentence would read without any punctuation but a period: "Mixed signals of transaction do not always distort the writer's intended meaning as much as a mixed signal of quantity, identity, or time might, but a reader will often get the feeling that something has gone wrong in the sentence without seeing exactly what it is a distraction no reader really needs." Like a sentence without a "just-to-clarify" comma (or parentheses), words run together and distort the sentence's sense of sequence.

Read it with the dash: "Mixed signals of transaction do not always distort the writer's intended meaning as much as a mixed signal of quantity, identity, or time might, but a reader will often get the feeling that something has gone wrong in the sentence without seeing exactly what it is—a distraction no reader really needs."

Many writers who appreciate how useful dashes are still have to hunt all over the keyboard for a "dash" key. Just go to the hyphen key and make two of them without any extra space.

The Seven Signals and the Standard Terms

This is a quick reference for locating the standard terms of English speech, grammar, and usage by their counterparts among the seven signals.

Quantity: Does the writer seem to mean *one or more than one*? A writer needs to clearly signal that by using the correct words or words' endings. The main culprits are pronouns and verbs, but adjectives, adverbs, and articles also proffer temptations for mixed signals here.

Time: *When* does the writer mean? People need to clearly signal time in a sentence. Time signals get mixed not only through errors in verb tense, but also by choosing prepositions that don't correctly "tell time."

Identity: *Who* does the writer seem to mean? One way or another, a writer will have to signal the identity of the person or persons he or she means. We do this by choosing the right pronoun, noun, capital letter, definite vs. indefinite article or adjective.

Location: *Where* does the writer seem to mean?" We have to clearly signal location one way or another. We do that with prepositions, adverbs of place, and certain adverbial phrases.

Transaction: "What does one side get from the other?" We have to show any exchanges that happen in a sentence. This could be an error in preposition choice, pronoun case, conjunction use, or use of the subjunctive mood.

Sequence: What *order* of words or thoughts does the writer seem to mean? One needs to clearly signal the sequence of words or thoughts. This oftentimes goes out of order with homophones, adjectives vs. adverbs, word forms, or through errors in parallel structure or syntax.

Relation: What *relation* of sentence parts does the writer seem to mean? Writers need to clearly signal how sentence parts relate to one another. This could be a fragment or run-on sentence; a certain type of error in subordination, coordination, or verb choice; or missing "added info." commas, as well as missing or misused possessive case, adverbs, or the subjunctive mood.

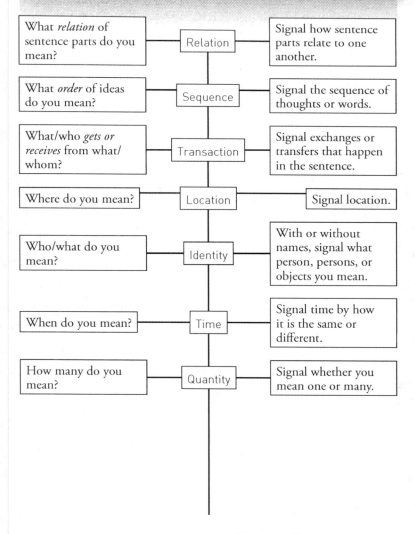

What *relation* of sentence parts do you mean?	Relation	Signal how sentence parts relate to one another.
What *order* of ideas do you mean?	Sequence	Signal the sequence of thoughts or words.
What/who *gets or receives* from what/whom?	Transaction	Signal exchanges or transfers that happen in the sentence.
Where do you mean?	Location	Signal location.
Who/what do you mean?	Identity	With or without names, signal what person, persons, or objects you mean.
When do you mean?	Time	Signal time by how it is the same or different.
How many do you mean?	Quantity	Signal whether you mean one or many.

If you already know the eight parts of speech and other grammatical terms and are familiar with the formal rules that apply them, this flow chart (sometimes called a "decision tree") may give you a view of how the seven signals of meaning correspond to traditional grammatical terms and rules. Take note of how the seven signals bridge over the differences between the terms.

The Formal Grammar Decision Tree

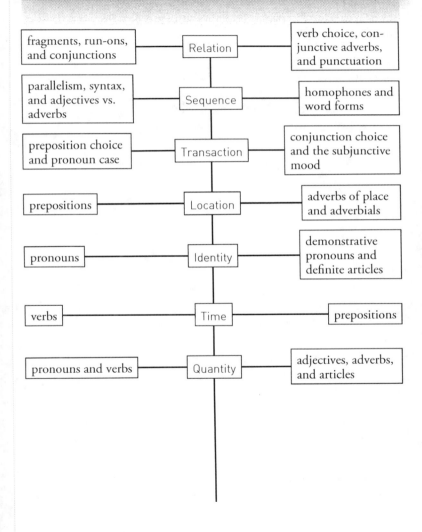

fragments, run-ons, and conjunctions	Relation	verb choice, conjunctive adverbs, and punctuation
parallelism, syntax, and adjectives vs. adverbs	Sequence	homophones and word forms
preposition choice and pronoun case	Transaction	conjunction choice and the subjunctive mood
prepositions	Location	adverbs of place and adverbials
pronouns	Identity	demonstrative pronouns and definite articles
verbs	Time	prepositions
pronouns and verbs	Quantity	adjectives, adverbs, and articles

Directions

1. Starting with the very last sentence on your page, check to see that you are fine in terms of quantity.
2. If it checks out well, go up to the next level, and check the sentence in terms of time.
3. Do the same as you work your way up through identity, location, transaction, sequence, and relation.
4. Once you've done this on one page of your writing, take notice of what mixed signals you needed to correct.
5. Make the best use of your time by concentrating only on those kinds of signals as you continue onto another page.

A Big Night for Pork

Here is the answer key to the first self-test in the chapter on Quantity. The solutions are in **bold**. Where more than one solution is possible, the possibilities are separated by slash marks (/).

Someone left **his or her/the** lights on in the supermarket parking lot. Meanwhile, all hell was breaking loose inside because the annual Pork-athon was in full swing, with each shopper filling up **his or her/a** cart with pork roasts, pork chops, pork sausages, and other cuts of suc-culent pig meat. On a night like that, **shoppers/people** could hardly be blamed for not being able to restrain themselves. **There are** many pictures to every story, so picture one group of petulant pork lovers fill-ing up eight carts each with the 16 lbs. **it was/ that were** allowed under the terms of the sale. **It's** not easy to blame them, considering how good lean pork would be good for their **health**. They even tried to cut into the checkout line, but a calm, self-assured **checker** put that gang of greasemongers in **its** place.

Here is the answer key to the second self-test in the chapter on Quantity. The solutions are in **bold**.

The Highway Patrol pulled us over outside of San Juan Capistrano (named for the patron saint of judges), just south of Los Angeles. After **the** officer collected ID's and ran warrant check**s** on everyone, he looked inside and saw that something didn't look quite right.

"You guys aren't really part of a church, are you?"

"Uh no, we're moving up to Sonoma," I said.

"Well, you don't have commercial plates, so you can't transpor**t** personal effects."

"We don't want to break the law, but here we are, and **this is** all the transportatio**n** we have right now. What can we do?"

The cop looked back down the road for a second and then at the bus. "The only way you can carry all **this stuff** in a vehicle of this type without commercial license plates is if it is a motor home. I'll tell you what, put a sign in the back window saying that **this** is a house vehicle, and I won't have to cite you."

We thanked him, and as he drove off, I took the cardboard backing out of **a** framed poster that somebody had packed between **his or her** dresser and a chest of drawer**s**, and made a sign. I used the edge of a **mattress** to brace the "House Vehicle" sign so it would face out of the back window. I had made **the** words large and the back window **was** about a foot above the motto the previous owner, a church, had painted on **the** back of the bus. Anyone driving behind us saw this:

House Vehicle

Follow Me to Sunday School

We had no further trouble from the law after that and started to make pretty good time, going up US 101 through Santa Barbara (named for the patron saint of mathematicians), past Santa Maria (news dealers), and San Luis Obispo (for the patron saint of Colombians). Two days, fifty gallons of gas, and half a **case** of brake fluid later, we made it to our new home, a farmhouse in Sonoma County, an hour north of San Francisco (the patron saint of zoos), and 30 minutes west of Santa Rosa (the **saint** for people ridiculed for their piety).

After making no headway in meeting the neighbors, it seemed the simplest way to avoid a bad **case** of social leprosy might just be painting the bus. I got a gallon of flat white house paint and painted the back and then went along the driver's side, where it said "PACIFIC BEACH CHURCH OF THE NAZARENE" in five-inch high black capital letters. I painted over five words and left "THE" just for the hell of it and kept on painting. As for the neighbors, they changed their impression of us after that.

Here are the solutions to "The News Commentary" in the Time chapter's self test. The solutions are in **bold**. Where more than solution is possible, the possibilities are separated by slash marks (/).

What **was** it/**could it have been** really like at Galileo's trial or Lincoln's *Gettysburg Address*? A lot of history's great events in the past **took/have taken** place a long time ago, but even relatively recent events **illustrate/ have illustrated** the problem of getting the complete picture of what it **was** like/**could have been like** to **be/have been** there. When we **see/ saw** a television news story about Bruce Springsteen's duet with Paul McCartney onstage at the Live Nation concert in London's Hyde Park just a few nights ago, we only **get/got** the images and sound that the video and audio equipment **captured/could capture/could have captured** and the words of news reporters who may **have/have been** or may not **have been** there. If we manage to find an audience member who **witnessed/had witnessed** the event in person, we might ask if the concert **was/had been** really loud enough to generate the noise complaints from residents living across the street at the far end of the park, which **were/had been** the complaints that the authorities had used in setting the strict curfew that prematurely **ended** the performance. Even if that person **heard/could have heard** the sound as it **bounced** off of the buildings, we **are left** to rely on someone else's personal impression of how it **felt/had felt**. Multiply that by dozens of journalists and television crews, newspaper photographers, hundreds of people who **took/ had taken** amateur videos of the concert, and thousands of the people who **listened** and **watched** from various parts of the concert area in the park, and we would still **be left** with an incomplete impression of what **happened/had happened** that night. We **will never get** a 100% complete impression because some small but important detail **escaped/will have escaped** the eyes and ears of those who **witnessed/had witnessed** the event, **did not get reported** at all or, if it **was witnessed/had been**

witnessed, got left/had gotten left out as not important enough to report. That **should make/should have made** us pause and wonder whether or not we **should assume/should have assumed** that people a century from now **will have gotten** an accurate impression of a major event in our own time.

This is the key to the self-test in the chapter on Identity. The questions have the same numbers they have as footnotes below "Virtual Identity and Real Language."

1. You would write what "this" could mean in this sentence, yes?

Well yes, since "this" clearly identifies itself as the word to be used for the example.

2. Okay, does "this" clearly signal identity this time?

"This" what, the rate at which students drop the class, the failure rate, or what happened in one of the face-to-face versions of the same classes? The writer has some explaining to do.

3. What does "it" mean in this instance?

What this "it" means is not clear at all, not without asking the writer anyway.

4. How about here?

In this case, "it" clearly means the state of being "unable to fathom computer software and have little success understanding detailed instructions when they ask for help."

5. The word "thing" is a stand-in for a more specific word, so which one?

In this case, "thing" is the reason why "it" happens in #4.

6. What does "that" mean?

It identifies how ". . . people in an unfamiliar situation are afraid of seeming dumb, especially in front of strangers" in the previous sentence.

7. What does "it" mean?

Here, "it" means the environment of the social networking sites.

8. Is this where a reader should ask the essay's author "Who do you mean?"

Yes, not all people pass themselves off that way, so who does the writer mean exactly?

9. Whose identity does this signal?

This is hard to tell since the nearest "them" is the people who "interact on social networking sites" way up in the previous paragraph. The author will need to identify who that is more specifically.

10. What identity does this signal?

"It" stands in for there being "more students who had trouble getting help posting their writing on the class site than there were students who had trouble getting help with improving their writing."

11. What about"this"?

It refers back to "it" in #10.

12. Is what "such" refers to clear in this sentence?

It could easily mean digital devices like computers, smartphones, tablets, but it would better to make certain by checking with the writer.

13. Is the same true of how "it" is being used here?

No, in this case, like in #4, "it" refers to a person's situation.

14. How clearly signaled is the identity of "them" here?

It is clear that "them" refers back to "people who seem to be able to quickly do anything on a computer, a smartphone, a tablet, and such" in the previous sentence.

15. Is the identity of what "it" actually refers to clear enough here?

It points back to "language" at the beginning of the sentence.

16. To what does "such" refer?

To answer a question with another question, who knows? It seems to have little to do with dialects or pages, so it's time to ask the writer, "What does 'such' mean here?"

17. Is this another place where a reader should ask the essay's author "who do *you* mean?

Yes it is. Someone who already knows what textese is would wonder "who do you mean?"

18. Does "that" as it is used here signal the same identity as "that" in the previous sentence?

No, it does not. The first "that" refers to what happens "When people have trouble with changing from one written dialect to another, they are either unaware of the correct one for the occasion or lack fluency in the right one." The second "that" means the college class that filled up.

19. What does "it" actually mean in this sentence, at least in terms of what thing "it" stands in for here?

There is no clue as to what "it" identifies in the sentence.

20. Are you ready to ask the writer "*what* 'which,' exactly"?

Who knows? Looking back at the previous sentences, the "which" in the sentence could identify a written dialect, being virtually popular, a medium of communication, or whatever "it" identifies in #19. If the writer wants clearer writing here, it's time for dialog with a reader.

Here are the solutions to "The Truth about Lying" in the Location chapter's self test. The solutions are in **bold**. Compare the solutions you see here with where you wrote "yes"or "no" next to a footnote below the self-test. Where more than solution is possible, the possibilities are separated by slash marks (/).

Everybody lies. I could be lying right now. A reader may now be wondering whether I am telling the truth **about/by** lying or lying **about/by** telling the truth. Actually I'm doing both. I'll lay this puzzle **at** the doorstep of rhetoricians since this what they might call a "rhetorical dilemma." I see that I should quickly define a few terms before I go any further. Rhetoricians are people who are fascinated with communication and they communicate that to anyone who cares, going **on** and **on** about the "who," "what," "how," "when," and "where" of people communicating. They especially like argument as a type **of** communication and love to argue about how other people argue. This may make rhetoricians seem like nervous, suspicious people, and things get worse when a rhetorical dilemma comes **along**. A dilemma is typically defined as a difficult problem, a kind of problem that has no easy solution and oftentimes involves a person being forced to make a bad choice **between/from among** two equally undesirable solutions, like having to choose **between** being told an unpleasant truth or being pleasantly deceived. A rhetorical dilemma has to do **with** the nature of the argument here.

Going back **to/into** everybody lying; it's no secret that everybody finds a reason not to tell the truth once **in** a while. "Everybody" is a term that naturally includes me. To illustrate, let me go to the old saying, "Tell me no secrets, and I'll tell you no lies." In other words, I will not lie to anyone who tells me anything I can freely pass **along to/on to** others, and I will lie to someone who tells me anything that I cannot pass **along to/on to** others. That means privacy has true value and lying is one of the ways people protect the bits of information that would become damaging **to** themselves or others if shared. It follows that I would only lie if the truth about everybody lying is a fact that needs to be kept secret. A good arguer defines the terms **of** argument. I've just defined three terms, and I'm not lying.

This is the key to the self-test in the chapter on Transaction. The solutions you would suggest to the writer are in **bold**.

In rugby, a player who plays on in spite of minor injuries earns bragging rights for **himself or herself**. A political blogger on the other hand, often begins with bragging and proceeds to inflict injuries upon people who are not there to defend themselves. A blog is shorthand for an online "web log" and it is typically where a "blogger" posts his or her thoughts and where readers respond. This makes blogging especially aggressive when the topic is politics, and political blogging seems like a kind of team sport with rough play much like rugby's because **in return** for subscribing to the blog, readers get to join the mayhem.

To compare rugby to blogging one last time, rugby is a physically tough game, mainly because its manner of play is very direct. A player gets the ball down the field past the opposing player at all costs, but the game requires that a player **have** a lot of knowledge before trying out for a team and **avoid** willfully inflicting injury **on whomever** else is in the game. If every political blogger **were** to follow that rule, the web would be a better place. The content of many political blogs is downright nasty, with cheap shots being the norm more than the exception.

It's fair to say that written arguments have been around a while. After all, this country was founded and then developed through a series of arguments, some directed **to whomever** could read them. But rational arguments are not what we always see posted on political blog websites. They seem to bring out the worst in some readers, as if typing nasty comments about politicians they don't like and other readers with **whom** they disagree passes for critical reasoning. Though some blogs are well reasoned, many others read as if the author prefers that a reader **remain** as uninformed about history, current events, and economics as possible, as if he or she **were** a newborn baby that had somehow been born literate. When it comes to responding to what they have read on a blog site, many political bloggers' readers seem to demand that ignorance of the facts **be** seen as a red badge of courage. Apparently a person doesn't always need to know very much to have an opinion these days.

This is the key to the self-test in the chapter on Sequence. The solutions you could suggest to the writer are in **bold**.

When I started college, I wanted to look a little more into it **than** other students because I believed that it wasn't only **me** helping **myself** succeed. I was a **serious student**, but the school seemed nothing like I had imagined it would be. No one could **have** imagined what a **strange** experience it would be for me.

During the first week of classes, the parking enforcement staff diligently responded to students' attempts at creative parking, towing **their** cars one by one. Fortunately, I didn't have to worry about parking at Big State University because I was able to take public transportation and get there **quickly. A lot** of the students were walking around like zombies. **Almost** none of them could find the classes they needed and just **seemed** disoriented and **desperate** as they lurched from one side of the campus to the other in pursuit of classes with empty seats.

Not that a seat in a classroom was anything special since the walls of one of my classrooms had pictures of the outside **where** there should **have** been windows. It turned out that I wasn't the only serious student in my classes. It turned out that a lot of the chatter in the back of the classroom was among students who were answering questions and **sharing** notes from the last class meeting. I was right about success not coming without the help of others.

Here is the answer key to the self-test in the chapter on Relation. The solutions are in **bold** in parentheses. Where more than one solution is possible, the possibilities are separated by slash marks (/).

Often thought of as "the beautiful people," celebrities appear on television, highway billboards, glossy magazine covers, and other places as well dressed, well groomed, and well, beautiful. More of these people are spotted in our local convenience stores and supermarkets than almost anywhere else on the planet, **(so/and)** my fellow Californians and I should divulge a dirty little secret. They don't look all that glamorous pushing their carts through the produce section or making a late-night stop for a half-gallon of milk. **(Join this incomplete next sentence to the sentence after it.)** Aside from the unnoticeable closed-circuit security camera. Celebrities need to look good in front of cameras, **(and/since/because/as)** that affects their ability to stay in the public eye. They have to look beautiful for commercial reasons. **(Join this incomplete next sentence to the previous sentence, or add "but" at the end, and join it to the sentence after it.)** Not to degrade the value of one of our state's biggest exports, right up there with pesticide-free lettuce, organic tomatoes, and hormone-free chicken breasts. The rest of the world should know that Hollywood types use the services of health spas (a.k.a. "fat farms") and migrant skin care workers who go to exfoliate, trim, or spray as needed. These services are available to the public, for a price of course, **(and)** most of us will admit to needing a little improving now and then.